HONESTY WITH GOD

HONESTY
with
GOD

Learning to Pray from the Psalms

DAN SCHAEFFER

Our Daily Bread
Publishing™

Requests for permission to quote from this book should be directed to: Permissions Department, Our Daily Bread Publishing, PO Box 3566, Grand Rapids, MI 49501, or contact us by email at permissionsdept@odb.org.

Scripture quotations, unless otherwise indicated, are taken from the New American Standard Bible®, copyright © 1960, 1971, 1977, 1995, 2020 by The Lockman Foundation. Used by permission. All rights reserved. www.Lockman.org.
    Poetry extracts from the New American Standard Bible have been set as prose throughout for ease of reading.

Scripture quotations marked MSG are taken from *The Message*, copyright © 1993, 2002, 2018 by Eugene H. Peterson. Used by permission of NavPress, represented by Tyndale House Publishers. All rights reserved.

Scripture quotations marked NKJV are taken from the New King James Version®. Copyright © 1982 by Thomas Nelson. Used by permission. All rights reserved.

Interior design by Hillspring Books, Inc.

ISBN: 978-1-64070-259-2

Library of Congress Cataloging-in-Publication Data Available

Printed in the United States of America
23 24 25 26 27 28 29 30 / 8 7 6 5 4 3 2 1

To my Lord and Savior, Jesus Christ,

revealed so powerfully to me in the Psalms.

May this book point others to you.

Contents

Chapter One

Honest to God

Approaching Him through the Psalms

A number of years ago, President Barack Obama and his wife, Michelle, traveled to England to meet with the British government officials. While there, they were scheduled to meet the queen. Much was written in the press about the proper protocol for meeting royalty. There were specific protocols of dos and don'ts. As a result, many eyes were on the Obamas when they were presented to the queen.

What caused a stir that resonated for weeks in the news was when Michelle broke protocol—when she was presented before the queen, Michelle gave her a hug. I'm sure there were many arched eyebrows and quiet gasps that filled the room. You aren't supposed to touch the queen! But later we learn from the queen's biographers and people close to her that she didn't mind it at all—in fact, she found it refreshing. It was a display of affection, and those were welcomed. She is still, after all, human.

One of the big questions for any religion that purports to approach God is, how do you talk to God? What attitude do you take toward Him? What kind of pose should you strike? What words do you use? What offends Him?

What pleases Him? What is He looking for from us? We certainly don't want to approach Him too casually, nor do we want to feel He is utterly unapproachable. But where is the balance, and how can we know? The most we could hope for is that we make a good guess.

Yet in the Bible, God has left us the Psalms, 150 wonderful examples of how to approach God safely. These are songs and poems inspired by God through various men to reveal, among other things, how God wants to be approached. In every psalm we hear someone speaking honestly to God—through the inspiration of the Scriptures.

In other words, we are hearing, reading, and singing the kinds of conversations God wants us to have with Him. And we will be amazed at how honest He wants us to be. He wants to hear not only our confession of faith and trust but also our doubts, fears, frustrations, sorrows, thanks, and joys.

In this book we will be looking at different psalms and learning through each of them how to approach God, how to speak to Him, and how to pray to Him in each and every season of life and faith. At the end of each chapter, there are a few questions to help you reflect and interact with what you've just read. In the Discussion and Reflection Questions section at the back of the book, you'll find more questions, further study, and action steps. But before we begin, let's learn about the Psalms in general, because they are fascinating.

The Background of the Psalms

In the Hebrew Bible, the book of Psalms (also known as the Psalter) means "the Book of Praises." It is often abbreviated to "Praises." Our word *psalms* comes from the Greek translation of the Hebrew title *psalmos*, which means "to touch or pluck a bowstring or a stringed instrument." Eventually it came to refer to a psalm or song of praise to God. They were first called psalms in the third century BC, when the Greek translation of the Hebrew Bible (the Septuagint) was put together.

For three thousand years the Psalms have been at the heart of the spiritual life of the people of God. The Psalms were the divinely inspired hymnbook for the public worship of God in ancient Israel.[1] Because psalms were sung and not merely read, they stayed with you and allowed you to remember them more easily. It is thought that Ezra the scribe collected and arranged all the Psalms—so the Psalter was actually formed 450 years before Christ.[2]

During the Middle Ages, the Psalms were the most familiar part of Scripture to most people precisely because they were sung. Not everyone could read, but everyone could remember a song. In fact, the Psalter was likely the only Scripture the average Christian might own.

Athanasius, the fourth-century church father, called the Psalms "an epitome of the whole Scriptures."[3] Martin Luther called the Psalms "a little Bible, and a summary of the Old Testament."[4] The Psalms weren't a theological textbook but a written example of the most vibrant and transparent worship imaginable. The hymnbook of the Old Testament, they later became the hymnbook of the early church.

The Psalms were considered so important that in the early church, a thorough knowledge of them was required to be ordained. The Second Council of Nicaea (AD 587) concluded that no one was to be appointed a bishop unless he knew the Psalter thoroughly. At the Eighth Council of Toledo in AD 653, it was ordered that no one could be promoted to any ecclesiastical position who did not know the entire collection of Psalms.[5]

And perhaps most important to us, the Psalms were the songbook of Jesus. It's likely Jesus would have sung all the Psalms constantly throughout His life, so He likely knew them by heart. It is the book of the Bible that Jesus quoted the most. Psalms were inspired poems, lyric poetry designed to expose the inner emotions of the composer. They were lyrical poems adapted to the harp or lyre and meant to be sung, not read.

The Psalms Weren't Always One Big Book

What many people don't know is that the Psalter wasn't always just one big book. The book of Psalms is actually five books combined together. The Psalms are a collection! One hundred are attributed to specific men; fifty are anonymous. They were put in collections by different editors at different times in history.

The five books are arranged this way:

Psalms 1–41 (book one)

Psalms 42–72 (book two)

Psalms 73–89 (book three)

Psalms 90–106 (book four)

Psalms 107–150 (book five)

At the end of every book is a closing doxology or benediction. So at the end of Psalm 41:13 we read, "Blessed be the LORD, the God of Israel, from everlasting to everlasting. Amen and Amen." Psalm 72:20 reads, "The prayers of David the son of Jessie are ended." Psalm 89:52 reads, "Blessed be the LORD forever! Amen and Amen." Psalm 106:48 reads, "And let all the people say, 'Amen.' Praise the LORD!" And the end of Psalm 150:6 reads, "Let everything that has breath praise the LORD. Praise the LORD!"

Interestingly, Bible teacher Harry Ironside, in his commentary on the Psalms, discerned that each collection of books had a theme. He also noticed that each of the first five books of the Bible, the Pentateuch, also had a theme, and noted the amazing similarities.

Psalms 1–41 have the theme of divine life and electing grace. The theme of Genesis was divine life and election.

Psalms 42–72 have the theme of redemption. Exodus has the theme of redemption.

Psalms 73–89 have the theme of sanctification—communion with God. The book of Leviticus has the theme of sanctification.

Psalms 90–106 have the theme of testing and trials. The book of Numbers has the theme of testing and experience.

Psalms 107–150 have the theme of the God who overrules—divine government. The book of Deuteronomy has the theme of divine government.[6]

The Pentateuch was written by one man, Moses, yet the Psalms were written by many men. But the Holy Spirit inspired them all.

The Purpose of the Psalms

According to Dr. John Goldingay, "The Bible assumes that we do not know instinctively how to talk with God but rather need some help with knowing how to do so."[7] How true!

Again, the Psalms were not primarily to be read the way we do today; they were meant to be sung. They were written to change the way we see and interact with God, so every situation imaginable shows up: fear, danger, resentment, anger, confusion, joy, thanksgiving, disappointment, and many more. And often you can find many of these emotions in one psalm. It's why author and pastor Timothy Keller has called the Psalms "the medicine chest for the heart and the best possible guide for practical living."[8]

As scholar Walter Brueggemann remarked in his book *The Message of the Psalms*, "The Psalms are helpful because they are a genuinely dialogical literature that expresses both sides of the conversation of faith."[9] In other words, we hear not only trust, faith, joy, and praise but also anger, doubt, anxiety, fear, and confusion.

And the Psalms are poetry, so they demand reflective reading. They are designed to arouse our emotions and stimulate our imaginations toward God, and poetry is more effective at that than plain prose. Theologian J. Sidlow Baxter says that the Psalms provide "for our emotions and feelings the same kind of guidance as the other Scriptures provide for our faith and actions."[10]

And when we read the Psalms, we are exposed to the many facets of God's beautiful and wonderful nature through metaphor and simile. We read that God is our shepherd, our king, our warrior, our mother, our father, our teacher, our judge, and so on. Too often we have a stuffed-shirt idea of God in our mind. We desperately need to see Him as He is. We need to see Him as tender as a loving mother, caring as a shepherd, strong like a warrior, and a judge who will one day deal with evil.

Baxter notes that the Psalms are "a river of consolation which though swollen with many tears, never fails to gladden the fainting. It is a garden of flowers which never lose their fragrance, though some of the roses have sharp thorns. It is a stringed instrument which registers every note of praise and prayer, of triumph and trial, of gladness and sadness, of hope and fear."[11]

But one of the primary things the Psalms are meant to do is to reveal Jesus. Many scholars have pointed out that certain passages in the Psalms are messianic—that is, they predict the coming Messiah. But more than that, they witness to Jesus and were meant to reveal Him even more. As Jesus told us in Luke 24:44, "These are My words which I spoke to you while I was still with you, that all things which are written about Me in the Law of Moses and the Prophets and the Psalms must be fulfilled."

Old Testament professor Bruce Waltke wrote, "It seems as though the writers of the NT are not attempting to identify and limit the Psalms that prefigure Christ, but rather are assuming that the Psalter as a whole has Jesus Christ in view and this should be the normative way of interpreting the Psalms."[12]

Scholar N. T. Wright goes even further: "Here is the challenge for those who take the New Testament seriously: try singing these psalms Christologically, thinking of Jesus as their ultimate fulfillment. See how they sound, what they do, where they take you." [13]

The early church used the Psalms in worship. It had been the hymnbook of the temple and the synagogues and became so for the church.

The Psalter was the songbook of Jesus!

Who Wrote the Psalms?

We know that David wrote perhaps seventy-three psalms, Solomon wrote several, the sons of Korah wrote twelve, Asaph wrote twelve, Heman the Ezrahite wrote one, Ethan the Ezrahite wrote one, and Moses wrote one.

The first two books are mainly psalms of David, the third is mainly by Asaph, the fourth is mainly anonymous, and the fifth is partly psalms of David and partly anonymous. The first book of Psalms was likely created by Solomon, the second by the Korahite Levites (Sons of Korah), the third by Hezekiah, and the fourth and fifth by Ezra and Nehemiah. So . . . it took over five hundred years to finish the Psalter we have today. [14]

Different Kinds of Psalms

There are many different types of psalms:

- hymns (songs of joy intended to be sung when everything was going great)
- laments (sung by those in distress)
- thanksgiving psalms (usually a response to some deliverance by God)
- confidence psalms (expressing confidence in God even when facing great trials)
- prophetic psalms (where God is the speaker, not the person facing danger or expressing joy or courage; they speak of our Lord)
- wisdom psalms (when a particular psalm reminds us of the Wisdom Books—Job, Proverbs, Ecclesiastes, and Song of Songs)
- remembrance psalms (looking back at great acts of God in the past on behalf of His people)
- royal psalms (songs that refer to God as King or to a human king)

- imprecatory psalms (which seem to speak of revenge and anger and malice toward an enemy)

In short, there are psalms to cover every human situation and emotion we can experience.

The Nature of the Psalms

As we have noted, the Psalms are lyric poetry, and as such they express the deep feelings we can have, and they find their source in the feelings and emotions of the writer. It's not something arrived at simply by mental thought. Psalms speak and articulate the deepest feelings in our heart. So they can be pensive, joyful, despairing, victorious, and more, all depending on the feelings and experiences of the author. The words can then be either sung or put to music.

The Psalms reflect the heart even more than the mind, and that is what makes them so special. When we speak of our trials and testings, we try to speak words of faith: "I know God will deliver me!" and "I know God is in charge and it will all work out."

In our American culture we are often embarrassed as Christians to share what we are really feeling out loud.

Sadness, anger, confusion, disappointment.

We are afraid that if we share too much of these, people might feel we are blaming God, or losing our faith, or abandoning God. Yet when we read the Psalms, we often read phrases and words we would be too embarrassed to say—but which we, too, really feel.

In a real sense, the Psalms give us permission to vent the feelings we guard closely. Sometimes we just can't understand what God is doing. We are disappointed. The God we had in our mind didn't show up. But those powerful emotions are important. They are a signal that there is something wrong not with God but with our understanding of Him. We aren't so much disappointed with the real God but with the God we had imagined Him to be.

While we are hesitant to complain to God, the Psalms aren't. They are breathtakingly and refreshingly honest. And on the flip side, joy and praise can well up inside us so powerfully that we are at a loss for words to express what we feel. Here again the Psalms come to our rescue. God gives us the words we often struggle with. He helps us to speak back to Him words of deepest pain and greatest joy. And when we do this, we enter the psalm itself.

We have many different emotions and feelings. Wouldn't it be nice to learn how to pray in a more honest and vulnerable way to your heavenly Father? And when you are confused and scared or disappointed with God, wouldn't it be nice to learn how to express those very real emotions to God—and yet not sin?

God Wants You to Know How to Talk to Him

That is the genius of the book of Psalms. God is saying, "Talk to me, and here, let me show you how." Isn't that awesome? God wants us to feel free to express our full gamut of emotions to Him and learn how to do it without sinning.

One of the greatest Christian fallacies is the idea that true faith and trust ignore situations and realities. Faith, we are told, blocks out negative thoughts and concentrates only on desired outcome. Yet time after time that idea is shattered in the Psalms. Not once will you see even a tinge of sugarcoating or blind faith. For faith in God to be real, it has to accept and recognize the real danger and obstacles it faces. Only when we truly realize the gravity of our situation can our faith in God be exercised.

> For faith in God to be real, it has to accept and recognize the real danger and obstacles it faces.

To deny the danger leads to denying the greatness of the deliverance. To put our faith in God even when we are confused, angry, or terrified is a far greater blessing to our Lord than pretending we aren't feeling those things. We do not honor God by pretending.

It's what Peter was referring to when he talked about the great inheritance we have been given by God, which is reserved in heaven for us, even though at present we are experiencing "various trials, so that *the proof of your faith, being more precious than gold* which is perishable, even though tested by fire, may be found to result in praise and glory and honor at the revelation of Jesus Christ" (1 Peter 1:6–7, emphasis added).

In a nutshell, you have here the template for many of the Psalms. Various trials occurred in the lives of the human authors, their faith was severely tested, but they believed by faith that God would deliver them. But they never denied the danger. The authors expressed what they felt, not what they should have felt. Isn't that comforting?

The Psalms Are Mirrors

When we identify with the psalmist, or the joy or trust of the psalmist, we then become the "I" of the psalm. We enter the psalm itself. Because we can do that, there is a psalm for every season of life. The Psalms give us 150 things we can say to God, and the author of the psalm can speak about a number of things within each psalm.

As John Goldingay paraphrases Athanasius, the church father, "Most of Scripture speaks *to* us; the Psalms speak *for* us." Goldingay adds, "The Psalms make it possible to say things that are otherwise unsayable. . . . The Psalter teaches not by *telling* us how to pray but by *showing* us how to pray" (emphasis added).[15]

I remember the first time I allowed myself to get really mad at God. I had been a Christian for many years and was a church-planting pastor. Our church was struggling with finances, and there was so much stress and disunity about the budget that it was consuming all my time and energy. This went on for months. It was miserable. And finally one day I couldn't take it anymore.

I remember praying angrily to God, "This isn't my job! This isn't what I signed up for. I can't control how much people give or don't give, and I don't want to. This is *Your* job, God! You are supposed to provide what we need. My job is to shepherd Your flock. I'm done worrying about this! If the church goes broke, it goes broke, but I'm done stressing about this!"

I had never done this before and was instantly remorseful. After all, I had been very direct and blunt with the Creator, but ironically, I suddenly felt peace. I sensed God saying gently to my spirit, "Good. Now we're both on the same page. Go do what I called you to do, and let me take care of the money."

And He always has. When the giving goes down, I don't get stressed, and when it goes up, I don't get excited. That's not my area. I'm a shepherd, not a banker.

Only later did I realize how God had choreographed that moment. I needed to get angry—because it caused me to finally be honest. We both wanted me to stop stressing about money and focus on shepherding. God was able to speak so powerfully and tenderly to me because I was finally being truly honest with Him. This was my first true personal psalm moment.

Do you believe that the Bible teaches that God will truly meet your needs? If you are a Christian, you will probably nod your head in the affirmative. Now, have you ever been stressed, wondering if God is actually *going* to meet your needs?

There is the truth we verbalize and the things we truly believe about God—they are not always the same. There is also the truth of our hearts—what we are actually *feeling* about God's truth at the moment. The Psalms allow us to express both of those realities at the same time, both conviction and faith, doubt and fear. Because we actually do feel those things at the same time.

Our faith in God can be strong, and yet because of some unique trial or experience, that belief is under more pressure than it has ever been. So David in the Twenty-Third Psalm can say, "Though I walk through the valley of the shadow of death, I will fear no evil. . . . You prepare a table before me in the presence of my enemies" (Psalm 23:4–5). David is affirming God is his protection, while at the same time experiencing real danger.

No posing.

When everything looks hopeless, we can learn how to approach Him.

When our confidence is shot and we realize we can't fix our lives, we can learn how to approach Him.

When we are completely confused about what He's allowing in our lives, we can learn how to approach Him.

And when we are overwhelmed with gratitude and in awe of what He has done for us, we can learn how to approach Him.

Honest to God! Isn't it about time *you* got honest with God?

QUESTIONS

1. What did you learn in this chapter about the Psalms that you didn't know before? How might this make you think of the Psalms differently in the future?

2. J. Sidlow Baxter wrote, "Psalms . . . provides for our emotions and feelings the same kind of guidance as the other Scriptures provide for our faith and actions." Do you ever feel that you need assistance knowing how to feel and respond toward God?

3. The Psalms teach us how to talk to God . . . without sinning! How is this an encouragement or even a relief to you?

Chapter Two

Setting Up a Living Trust

Psalm 4

My wife Annette's grandparents were a thrifty couple. They worked hard and were content with a simple life. They didn't indulge in many extravagances, and so they always had more money than month, as we say.

Being sharp, they invested a lot of money in blue-chip stocks, funds, and bonds. As a result of doing this for many years, they had a small fortune laid by when they were old. When they were older and in poor health, they realized that a great part of their assets would be eaten up in taxes upon their death and not be available for their only daughter, Rosalie. As a result, they were advised by estate lawyers to set up what is called a living trust.

A living trust is a legal document through which your assets are all placed into trust for your benefit during your lifetime, and they can more easily be transferred to your beneficiaries upon your death, while avoiding large tax hits. It is what enabled Annette's grandparents to leave their daughter the bulk of their estate when they passed away.

As a result, they got to benefit not just their only child, but through her, all five grandchildren as well. A living trust benefits not only the person who has one but also those they might want to leave it to in the future. This psalm is going to show us that God has set up a living trust for each of His children as well.

The Benefits of a Living Trust

In the Psalms we are frequently aware that the psalmist is facing a very real, very specific problem we aren't privy to. We are rarely told what it is. At first that seems strange, but we need to remember that the Psalms were written to serve as model prayers and hymns for other worshippers. We all struggle with something, and the specific issue isn't important—how we need to respond to it is. That's how the Psalms help us. We learn how to approach Him.

You will notice that Psalm 4 is an "evening prayer of trust in God." We are being called to a living trust, but trust is only engaged when it faces trouble and difficulty. And it is at night that our fears are magnified, aren't they?

As a young pastor planting a church, I learned this lesson powerfully. Planting a church is a daunting task, and a great many church plants fail. I was very aware of this, and it caused me anxiety.

I would have many concerns and worries about church and wake up in the middle of the night, stressed and unable to sleep. In an attempt to diminish my anxieties, I would go into my office (which was in our home) and try to come up with a solution to these problems. I would be in there several hours. But inevitably I would be convinced I had found the solution to the great problem and could go back to sleep. I was tired a lot in those days!

I wasn't trusting in the Lord—I was trusting in Dan Schaeffer's ability to fix the problem because, after all, wasn't that what I was being paid to do? Wasn't that my job? And yet every single time I woke up in the morning and remembered my fear of the night before, I would think, What was I so worried about? That fear was no longer powerful and debilitating. Night had taken a normal concern and magnified it all out of proportion. Night does not create our fears, but it can magnify them.

Perhaps that's why Proverbs 3:25 tells us, "Do not be afraid of sudden fear nor of the onslaught of the wicked when it comes."

Our History with God

Answer me when I call, O God of my righteousness! You have relieved me in my distress; be gracious to me and hear my prayer. (v. 1)

A strange thing is happening here—David, the author of Psalm 4, is asking God to answer him in some area of anxiousness but then immediately follows that up with, "You have relieved me in my distress." One is a present-tense problem; the other is a past-tense experience. Don't miss this. David is approaching God with a new problem, a new stress, but instantly confesses the reason he is approaching God at all: "You have relieved me in my distress." David and God had history. And so do you and God.

You can never grow in your trust of God unless you learn to continually remember all the ways God has already helped you in your past. Right now you have a problem, anxiety, obstacle, or issue you are facing, and it is stressing you. You aren't sure what's going to happen—that's the source of your anxiety. You imagine the worst—which makes it worse.

Don't you wish you *didn't* imagine the worst?

We need to learn to get historical with God. We need to reach into our past when we were also stressed but where God met us and delivered us. Think of all the things you worried about . . . that never happened. How many times have you called out for His help, and He has helped you? That's what David is getting at. David had a mental journal of God's faithful acts of deliverance toward him.

David was using his *history* with God to gain *confidence* in God. That's what we need to learn to do. He knew that God would do what He had done before: "Be gracious to me and hear my prayer." God had done it before and would do it again, of this David was sure.

Now David shifts gears and allows us to see some of his stress. People were making accusations against him and seeking his harm.

O sons of men, how long will my honor become a reproach? How long will you love what is worthless and aim at deception? Selah. (v. 2)

The things they should have honored David for, they were mocking and ridiculing him for. These were other Hebrews, David's own people. But they didn't all have David's walk with God. One of the sad realities of life is that you can be completely innocent of what other people accuse you of but know that you are never going to change their minds about you. They will not allow the facts to get in the way of their preconceived opinions. In short, you will always be the target of their frustration.

They were saying, "Stop talking about your faith and your special relationship with God all the time, David! Stop with all the morality and holiness—no one loves a holier-than-thou person."

We are reminded that to tie your happiness to human approval is a no-win scenario. Jesus was always being misunderstood, which led to criticism and distrust. Once someone doesn't trust you, everything you say and do is suspect. People criticize us even when we have actually acted with great integrity. It's not new.

The Disloyalty of Stuff

"How long will you love what is worthless and aim at deception? Selah" (v. 2). As David observed their lives, he saw them chasing things that weren't worth chasing. He is saying, "You are chasing things that will never be faithful to you." The things in life we chase have no loyalty to us. I have friends and families that no matter what happens to me will stick by me and be loyal to me. My stuff is another matter.

My house doesn't care who lives in it. My money doesn't care who spends it. My cars couldn't care less who drives them. Even my reputation, given the right circumstances, would desert me in a New York minute. My influence in life can be gone like dew in a heat wave. All these things are unfaithful. It is foolish to love things that can't remain faithful to you. They are worthless. So a "selah," a pause, is introduced here. Think about this. Dwell on it.

But know that the LORD has set apart the godly man for Himself;
the LORD hears when I call to Him. (v. 3)

David wasn't in the line of kings—he had been set apart by God through the prophet Samuel. He wasn't in the monarchy of Saul or his line. So people who loved Saul and were loyal to his line would always resent David. David is saying, "God set me apart, as He sets apart every godly man or woman for Himself. As a result, 'the LORD hears when I call to Him.'"

As Christians, we too, have been "set apart for God." Peter reminds us, "You are a chosen race, a royal priesthood, a holy nation, a people for God's own possession, so that you may proclaim the excellencies of Him who has called you out of darkness into His marvelous light" (1 Peter 2:9).

In 2 Chronicles 16:9, we are reminded that "the eyes of the LORD move to and fro throughout the earth that He may strongly support those whose heart is completely His." These are the benefits of a living trust. God hears us when we call.

The Dangers of Rejecting a Living Trust

David tells you that when trouble, loss, and disappointment come into your life, and when you are frustrated,

> Tremble, and do not sin. Meditate in your heart upon your bed, and be still. Selah. (v. 4)

Yes, you are frustrated with God in some way, but don't let that frustration turn into sin. Don't let your anxiety cause you to turn to some other idol, to lead you to find some other kind of savior. Don't put your hope in what is worthless. Think about God, meditate upon His power, love, and goodness to you.

He doesn't say meditate upon your problem but rather meditate upon God. Let your fears and frustrations draw you near to God. "Be still!" That's the pose of trust, quiet confidence in God. It's the best thing to do when you are stressed—it's also the hardest. We so desperately want to feel like we don't need a Savior, that we can handle all our problems by ourselves.

We struggle to believe God has it all under control, so we don't want to give up personal control. But it's so essential. So we have another "selah." Pause and think here. God knows we struggle with this, so He asks us to pause and ponder this more deeply.

> Offer the sacrifices of righteousness, and trust in the LORD. (v. 5)

David is saying that as you are being still before God, let Him search your heart and show you sins you may be entertaining. Seek His righteousness. If you realize there is a sin that has a hold on you, sacrifice up your sin so that it might die and you can live . . . in peace.

Our dog will occasionally get a tick from the weeds she runs through, and she can't reach it to get rid of it. As long as a tick or flea has a host, it will live off it. It will continue to suck its blood, introduce infections, and weaken it. So we get out our tweezers and remove it. But we have to be careful to remove all the tick. Any part left can fester and cause an infection.

Sin is like a spiritual tick that attaches itself to you. It will suck the joy out of your life and block God's blessing to you. You must remove it, but you must remove it all—you can't hope to just remove some of it, or all of it for just a while. It has to die. You have to evict it, kill it, remove it. And you can't do that unless you "trust in the Lord," because we have to believe that God is more precious and fulfilling to us than the sin we are holding on to.

> We have to believe that God is more precious and fulfilling to us than the sin we are holding on to.

We often trust some sin or pleasure to give to us, or be to us, what only God can do or be for us. Sin dilutes our trust because we are treating that sin or pleasure as our new savior. We obey its every command.

Many are saying, "Who will show us any good?"
Lift up the light of Your countenance upon us, O Lord! (v. 6)

Here David recounts in his song to God what David's enemies have been saying to him. They were questioning the promises of God that David was always trumpeting. He echoes those back to God.

"When is life going to get better like you claim it will? What is going to make it better? Tell us, David. After all, you seem to have all the answers." David's response is, "Lift up the light of Your countenance upon us, O Lord!"

Look to the Lord

In our society, advertisers spend billions each year trying to show us what is good. "*This* is what's good. *This* is the cure for what ails you!" We call them commercials.

> Are you miserable, like Dwayne here? It's quite likely that you need our new drug. Look how sad Dwayne was before, and look how happy he is now! *This* is the good you have been looking for!

> Do you want to feel young and sexy and adventurous? Well, you can— if you buy this new car! Look at this young, sexy, and adventurous person who is happy in their new car! Get the car. *It* will be the good you have been looking for!

> Do you want to have attractive friends, go to lots of classy parties, and frolic on the beach in the company of happy, smiling, laughing people? Buy our beer! *It's* the good you've been looking for.

Advertisers have learned that what we really want is not the product but the *experience* the product promises. We want the joy beneath the thing, so they promise us that if we get the product, we'll also get the feeling.

When you are looking to salve the deepest part of your soul, nothing physical can accomplish that. None of the things they advertise are able to reach that deep into your soul. They are all topical ointments, good for mild amusements or temporary happiness—but they quickly lose potency. You are trying to treat a spiritual hemorrhage with Band-Aids and ointments that can only touch you at the shallowest level. We need the face of God to smile upon us.

Final Arguments for a Living Trust

> You have put gladness in my heart,
> more than when their grain and new wine abound. (v. 7)

As believers we don't need to depend upon things we can buy or own to make us happy and give us peace. That's why, with or without those things, we can have "gladness" in our hearts. Who put that gladness in David's heart? This is critical. It wasn't a *what*. It wasn't some *thing* that put joy in David's heart. It was *Someone* who put joy in David's heart.

The human soul can't find true peace and gladness if all it has for fuel is stuff, even really great stuff. It needs something that touches him or her at the deepest level—something not based on circumstances or privilege or good fortune. As humans, we desperately need to be touched at a deep level to be truly happy. We literally ache at times for that touching.

In fact, unbeknownst to so many, that's what we're really looking for when we chase money, things, success, relationships, and popularity. We are looking for and chasing that deep touching. We were made to need and desperately want that deep touching. But here is the thing: only God can touch us there—only He can reach that deep into us.

The Need for Something Deeper

Sometimes when times are hard and I'm discouraged and low, I sit on my couch and look over at Annette. And I am touched so deeply knowing that no matter what happens, she loves me. I have one deeply beautiful thing to touch and be helped by. God put her in my life for that purpose. I've told people, and I mean it, that if I lost everything, literally everything, and ended up living in a cardboard box in a dump, I could be happy if Annette were in that box with me.

But as wonderful as Annette is, and as much as I see how much God loves me through her, I need something even deeper. Annette could be taken from me. She is a beautiful gift, but what I really need is the even more beautiful Giver of the gift. Annette is a reflection of God's love to me. I need to touch the source, to know it's real, and to experience it. And I have. That can't be taken away from me. And that's why I can say, like David,

In peace I will both lie down and sleep, for You alone,
O Lord, make me to dwell in safety. (v. 8)

On the other hand, David's acquaintances can't. They only have one thing to try to bring them joy. While David has that deep, deep joy, their happiness is only found "when their grain and new wine abound" (v. 7).

Grain is the necessity of life, food, sustenance. We can be content when we have the basics of life. *New wine* is the luxury of life. We can be happy when we get new things, new stuff, new relationships—all the things this life promises will make us happy. But none of these will make anyone be able to "lie down and sleep" in peace, like David.

That's his point. His trust allows him to "dwell in safety" (v. 8). We can have peace when that deep ache within us has been met by the Lord. The greatest danger we face is not to our body—it's to our soul. We can have all that life promises will bring us joy, all the grain and new wine, and be miserable. And we can have few of those things but have the peace of God, and lie down and sleep the slumber of trust.

Most of us wouldn't really care what kind of danger we faced if we could be promised that we would not be afraid, that we'd be at perfect peace in spite of the danger. Would we really care if we lost health, home, usefulness, or status if we could be assured that we would be at peace with it all, that we would be happy and content anyway? I argue that we wouldn't. What we dread is the feeling of fear and anxiety. What we fear, as president Franklin Delano Roosevelt so wisely said once, is "fear itself." [1]

Ironically, we spend so much of our lives consumed with protecting our bodies, when what we need far, far more is protection for our souls. Our feelings and emotions want so desperately to be at peace. Our minds want to be at peace. We want to feel safe. A nearby danger isn't a threat to us if we know and feel we are safe from it.

When we go to zoos or aquariums, we are often only a few inches of strong glass away from a predator that would quickly and gladly end our lives. But we feel totally safe. Yes, there is danger nearby, but I feel safe. It's not the presence of the danger that is the problem—it's the feeling of danger that we dread.

We return to the need for the deep, deep touch in our soul—that touching and assuring and confidence we can only receive from God.

Where Is Jesus in Psalm 4?

David writes, "O sons of men, how long will my honor become a reproach?" (v. 2). In Matthew 11:19 Jesus said, "The Son of Man has come eating and drinking, and they say, 'Behold, a gluttonous man and a drunkard, a friend of tax collectors and sinners!' Yet wisdom is vindicated by her deeds." Jesus's honor became His reproach as well.

In John 8:41 Jesus said to the priests and scribes, "'You are doing the deeds of your father.' They said to Him, 'We were not born of fornication.'" When Jesus was conceived by the Holy Spirit of God, it was an honor, a divine birth, and yet it became His reproach in the eyes of men.

David also writes, "How long will you love what is worthless and aim at deception?" (v. 2). Jesus, speaking to the scribes and Pharisees in Matthew 23:4–7, said,

> They tie up heavy burdens and lay them on men's shoulders, but
> they themselves are unwilling to move them with so much as a finger.
> But they do all their deeds to be noticed by men. . . . They love the
> place of honor at banquets and the chief seats in the synagogues, and
> respectful greetings in the market places, and being called Rabbi by
> men.

Jesus saw people loving what was worthless and aiming at deception, and, like David, called them out.

David writes, "The Lord hears when I call to Him" (v. 3). In John 11:40–43, after Lazarus had died and the memorial service was being held, Jesus showed up. When He commanded that they remove the stone behind which Lazarus's dead body lay, He said,

> "Did I not say to you that if you believe, you will see the glory of
> God?" So they removed the stone. Then Jesus raised His eyes, and
> said, "Father, I thank You that You have heard Me. I knew that You
> always hear Me; but because of the people standing around I said it,
> so that they may believe that You sent Me." When He had said these
> things, He cried out with a loud voice, "Lazarus, come forth."

Jesus knew His Father heard when He called to Him.

Lastly, David writes, "Offer the sacrifices of righteousness and trust in the Lord" (v. 5). And the author of Hebrews tells us Jesus did just that. Hebrews 7:26–27 says, "For it was fitting for us to have such a high priest, holy, innocent, undefiled, separated from sinners and exalted above the heavens; who does not need daily, like those high priests, to offer up sacrifices, first for His own sins and then for the sins of the people, because this He did once for all when He offered up Himself."

Jesus offered up the sacrifices of righteousness and trusted in the Lord. His life was the perfect sacrifice, and His trust was perfect in His Father. Jesus is all over Psalm 4.

Can we approach God this way? Can we ask Him to answer us when we call? Can we ask Him to be gracious and hear our prayers? Can we honestly share with God what evil people are saying about us—and doing to us? Can we remind God of what He has already done for us?

Notice how David's psalm speaks to God the way we would speak to a good friend. We aren't telling God anything He doesn't already know, but we are entering a real conversation with God. In the Psalms, we are encouraged to enter the psalm and be the "I" of the psalm, remember?

God wants you to speak with Him—and He's showing you how to do it without sinning. What is it you need to say to God?

QUESTIONS

1. We each have a history with God—times when He has helped us, guided us, rescued us, and protected us. Try to think of some times when you were afraid something bad was going to happen, and you prayed and stressed about it, and yet it didn't actually occur. How can we gain confidence in God using our history with God? What are you stressed about today?

2. The psalmist talks about loving "what is worthless and aiming at deception" (Psalm 4:5). The things we chase in life have no loyalty to us. What are some things in your life that you may be chasing that are actually worthless?

3. To truly be happy, we need to be touched at the deepest level of our soul. Share some things that have touched you that deeply.

Chapter Three

Sin and Its Discontents

Psalm 6

I want to talk about something that's happened to all of us at one time or another, and if it hasn't . . . just wait—it will.

You've blown it. You've done something really stupid, inconsiderate, and hurtful. And the worse thing is that you did this to someone you really cared about, someone who was crucial to your happiness. When you said or did that hurtful thing, their expression changed, their body language changed, and their eyes might have filled with pain, maybe tears. They turned away physically, maybe emotionally. And suddenly everything in your world had changed.

You are still around them all the time, but now it feels different. You're tense, awkward, uncomfortable around them. You have trouble looking at them, trouble talking to them. Your appetite is gone. Your stomach is churning. You're tired all the time. You're getting depressed. You're getting angry—at yourself, at the situation, at life, at God. Your emotional pain has made you physically sick.

That relationship and its fracture is the number one thing in your life right now. It consumes your heart and mind. You want things to be like they were before, but you know you really hurt that person you love. You would do anything to get things back to normal.

But can you? Will you ever enjoy life again? Will you ever smile and laugh again? Will life ever be pleasant again? You really wonder. Because it doesn't seem like it ever will. A relationship that was crucial to your happiness is fractured and wounded.

We've all experienced this. At times we hurt when we should heal, we scold when we should forgive, we walk away when we should walk toward. And we're thinking primarily of our relationship with another person. But there is another personal relationship even more important than the one we are focused on. It's our relationship with God.

Our actions have offended God. We've grieved Him. We've created distance between Him and us emotionally and spiritually. The relationship that is most crucial to our happiness as humans, we have fractured and wounded. Now we miss the sense of His pleasure and presence. How can we get it back? What do we tell God? What do we share with Him?

This is the subject of Psalm 6.

Experiencing the Spiritual and Emotional Toll of My Sin

When we disobey God, when we walk away from Him, we can be blind to the fact that much of the suffering and stress we are enduring in life is coming as a direct result of that sin. We don't even consider that what we are enduring is connected to our relationship with our God and His purposes to draw us back to obedience through discipline. We can think it's just random trouble. But David knew better.

Every child of God, even though he or she has been given the perfect righteousness of Christ as a gift by faith, is still powerfully conscious of our daily failures. And the closer we walk with God, the more keenly we become aware of those failures.

When you first get married, you are aware that your spouse is not perfect, but the longer you are married, the more keenly aware you become of that imperfection. And this is a direct result of growing closer to them. It's the same with your relationship with God. In His perfect presence, we more keenly feel our shortcomings and failures.

Sometimes we forget the advantages we have over the Old Testament saints, like David. They understood God's grace and mercy—but not to the extent that we do. They looked upon an innocent lamb sacrificed to atone for their sin and saw God's grace toward them clearly, but not perfectly. We, on the other hand, can today look upon the Lamb of God and see Jesus and God's grace and mercy with absolute clarity. The blurriness is gone.

We realize who the Lamb was and what God did through Him and how, because of what Jesus did, we are completely forgiven and accepted. We realize that all of God's wrath toward our sins, past, present, and future, has already been satisfied forever. We see His grace in high definition. The Old Testament saints didn't see it quite that clearly. They could still fear that through their actions and sins, they were going to receive God's wrath and anger and punishment.

A Deep and Desperate Love

Lord, do not rebuke me in Your anger, nor chasten me in Your wrath. (v. 1)

Today we can see discipline in our lives as the loving hand of our heavenly Father conforming us to the image of Christ. We know our sins have already been judged, but sometimes loving discipline can feel like anger and wrath even when it's not.

As parents we can see our children doing something dangerous and get angry with them momentarily. They can run into the street without looking, play with sharp objects, or get ready to drink something dangerous, and we get angry with them and demand they stop instantly. But our anger comes from a deep and desperate love. We want them to be safe. Yet at the moment all our children can see is our anger. They are too young and immature to understand that the anger comes from that deep and desperate love.

It's the same with God, except that unlike us, God can't overreact. He brings discipline in our lives to help us—to keep us safe, to walk us back from a dangerous activity or attitude. At the moment all we can see is the discipline. It may not feel loving even though it is. Though David realizes that God has every right to rebuke and punish him, he only asks that God set a limit to it because it feels like it will never end.

And again we aren't told what the sin is. These psalms were written so they could be applied by everyone. And *everyone* has a sin standing between them and God. It's possible that in some way David had sinned and God was using his enemies to discipline him, as we will see at the end of the psalm.

For a king it might have involved powerful personal enemies within his country or national enemies with their armies. Sometimes God uses other people and circumstances to bring discipline into our lives, to bring discontent so that we want to move away from the sin and toward God.

> Be gracious to me, O Lord, for I am pining away; heal me, O Lord,
> for my bones are dismayed. And my soul is greatly dismayed. (v. 2)

Notice that David doesn't ask God to be fair. He doesn't ask for justice nor claim that he was innocent.

He asks for mercy and grace.

So often pressures and stress in our lives produce real physical suffering. Stress can cause headaches, indigestion, high blood pressure, fatigue, skin rashes, pain, sleeplessness, lack of appetite, and much more. If your problems suddenly disappeared, it's likely so would some of these symptoms.

About ten years ago, during a difficult time of life and ministry, I developed heart palpitations. I visited my doctor, who checked my heart, gave me a battery of tests, and then sat me down and said, "Your heart is fine. You're too stressed. This is all stress induced." I didn't believe him. I wondered what was really causing them. But it so happened that I had a sabbatical scheduled right about that time. In those three months away from the pressures of work and ministry, my heart palpitations disappeared.

Go figure.

David's sin had prompted God to bring suffering into his life, and that had then caused stress and the physical suffering that accompanies stress. David's enemies, and their actions, were stressing him out. He was *pining*, which means "to lose vigor, health, or flesh (as though through grief); to yearn intensely and persistently, especially for something unattainable."[1] He asks to be healed, because his bones are dismayed. This was a metaphorical way of saying, "I'm really sick. The problems I'm facing have devastated me physically." His soul, the part of him that feels and loves and worries and frets, is just devastated.

Whispered Prayers

But You, O LORD—how long? Return, O LORD, rescue my soul; save
me because of Your lovingkindness. (vv. 3–4)

David is so overcome that he cuts short his speech. He meant to ask, "How
long will you withhold your mercy?" but he never finished the sentence. I get
this. A number of times in my past when I have been laboring in prayer for
God's help in a desperate situation, my prayers eventually get shorter, until I'm
just whispering five words: "Lord, please help me, please."

It was all I had left to say. All the feelings I had were condensed into those
five words. Those five words were distilled and concentrated. They contained
all my energy, passion, and hope. No spiritual posing, no sermons, no mono-
logues, just "Lord, please help me, *please.*" And every time, God heard, and
every time, He rescued me.

Every time.

David knows that by his actions or words, he has caused God to turn away
from him, so he begs the Lord to *return* to him, not because he deserves it, but
because he needs it.

Every once in a while in a movie or book, you come across a scene in which
the villain, who has been trying to destroy or kill the hero, suddenly finds himself hanging onto a cliff for dear life. The only one available to rescue them is,
of course, the hero—the one they have been trying to destroy.

We all know the hero has every right to let the villain fall, but invariably
he rescues the villain, thus displaying his good character over the villain's bad
character. And the villain goes away grateful but ashamed. And this is how
David knows he must approach God. We sin against God, not the other way
around. And when we are in peril, we can dare to ask for rescue, not because of
our own character and virtue but because of God's. "Save me because of Your
lovingkindness" (v. 4).

David wants the relationship with God he had before he sinned. The discontents of sin had taken a terrible toll on his life and joy. Then David says,

For there is no mention of You in death; in Sheol who will give You
thanks? (v. 5)

Sheol was the place of the departed dead. Again, the Old Testament saints didn't have the full knowledge of what happened after death that we do. Today we know that when we die as Christians, we go straight into the presence of our Lord Jesus, where we can continue to praise Him (2 Corinthians 5:6–8).

But in another way, David could be saying, "Lord, if you rescue me in this life here and now, I will be able to praise you before the people appropriately, and many may be changed on account of Your marvelous rescue of me. If I just go to my death, that may not happen." Today we might say, "Lord, a live streamed praise session of Your rescue of me will be heard by many who can be changed by it. But if I die now . . . not so much."

Enduring the Physical Consequences of My Sin

C. S. Lewis wrote in his book *The Problem of Pain*, "Mental pain is less dramatic than physical pain, but it is more common and also more hard to bear. The frequent attempt to conceal mental pain increases the burden: it is easier to say, 'My tooth is aching,' than to say, 'My heart is broken.'"[2]

> I am weary with my sighing; every night I make my bed swim,
> I dissolve my couch with my tears. My eye has wasted away with
> grief; it has become old because of all my adversaries. (vv. 6–7)

David is worn out with sighing, with the futility of the situation. "Every night I make my bed swim." Ever spend the night crying? Ever been so miserable, so heartbroken, that your tears dampened your pillowcase? If so, you aren't alone. Great saints of God—great men and women of the faith—have spent time crying the night away.

Aren't the Psalms comforting?

A Diet of Tears

In Psalm 42:3 David writes, "My tears have been my food day and night, while they say to me all day long, 'Where is your God?'" In a different circumstance, David is crying again. But when we get to the New Testament, we get the same story. In Acts 20:18–31 Paul is speaking to the Ephesian elders, whom he is never going to see again. In verses 18–19, he said, "You yourselves know, from the first day that I set foot in Asia, how I was with you the whole time, serving the Lord with all humility *and with tears, and with trials* which came upon me" (emphasis added).

In verse 31 again he wrote, "For a period of three years I did not cease to admonish each one with tears." Both David and Paul and many other prophets and saints had something in common. They were weepers.

Jeremiah was called the Weeping Prophet. David is saying that his tears were like a river he had to swim through they were so heavy. Hot, salty tears were common to David. And here we realize that it's OK to cry, especially when you have a good reason to. Part of real prayer for us, at times, might involve tears. That's not a weakness. God feels and welcomes those tears.

There are pressure cookers that were designed to cook food faster at very high temps, and they do, but there is also a release valve at the top so that when the pressure gets too great in the pan, it will release steam and keep the pot from exploding and causing great damage. God knows that when we get so stressed and anxious, we need a release valve, and so He gave us crying, tears. And in His Word, He reminds us that it's appropriate to come before Him that way.

Crying is our relief valve. It helps us deal with the incredible pressure that can build up inside us at times. And it's amazing how a really good cry, even with sobbing, can bring a release of tension and a sense of calm. American culture isn't really comfortable with that, especially among men. But Semitic culture wasn't uncomfortable with it at all.

David was a weeper. It wasn't that he was more emotional than we are. He just wasn't embarrassed about *showing* his emotions like we are. David was a man's man, a mighty warrior, a John Wayne's John Wayne—but he wasn't in the least embarrassed about his tears. And maybe that's what God needs you to know today.

When you are frustrated, confused, and hurt, and your heart is breaking, it's OK to have a good cry. While being raised we were often told "Crying doesn't help anything." Actually, it does. It relieves tension. And it's honest. Real tears are a portrayal of the heart's true condition.

> When you are frustrated, confused, and hurt, and your heart is breaking, it's OK to have a good cry.

"My eye has wasted away with grief; It has become old because of all my adversaries" (v. 7). You may not know this, but when we are severely stressed and anxious, high levels of adrenaline in the body can cause pressure on the eyes, resulting in blurred vision. People with long-term anxiety can suffer from eye strain all day long. When we get old, our eyesight dims naturally. But this wasn't that. "It has become old because of all my adversaries."

Tim Keller wrote, "It often takes an experience of crippling weakness for us to finally discover [God's blessing]. That is why so many of the most God-blessed people limp as they dance for joy."[3]

No one who has not been profoundly terrified and forsaken prays profoundly. In other words, our fears and trials teach us to pray honestly and powerfully to God. Charles Spurgeon wrote, "Soul trouble is the very soul of trouble."[4] What he meant was that our worst troubles are those that affect us emotionally and spiritually—not just physically.

David's adversaries would normally bring out the warrior in him, but he realizes that this pain and suffering is coming from God as a result of some sin in his life. That changes things. And he is suffering internally, and that is causing real physical distress in his body.

Reaching for the Promised Grace

While the suffering and stress and anxiety that sin produced in David were powerful, even more powerful was David's understanding that God would not leave him that way, that God would not allow his enemies to dance victoriously over him.

While David is writing his psalm of lament, God gives him what some have called "an answering touch." It's the reminder that God is listening and will rescue him. Sometimes when we are really discouraged and there are no positive signs on the horizon, God graciously gives us a period of calm and peace in the midst of our storm.

We are suddenly emotionally at peace and content—when, given the circumstances, we really shouldn't be. We've been given unexpected strength in that moment to be "anxious for nothing, but in everything by prayer and supplication with thanksgiving let your requests be made known to God" (Philippians 4:6). And when we do that, we experience the "peace of God, which surpasses all understanding" (v. 7). It is an unnatural and divine peace. It is grace for the moment.

Peace instead of Protection

The storm isn't gone from our lives, but we are placed in the eye of it. It swirls around us, but we are protected in our hearts because we *know* God is going to rescue us. The fear can no longer debilitate us. And that's all any of us really want anyway. It's not what happens to us that is our greatest problem, but how we react to it.

Imagine your house burning down in a fire. Suddenly everything is gone— all your possessions, all your valuables, so many precious mementos—all gone. All you can see now is the loss, the devastation, the bad hand you've been dealt. You rage; you cry; you get depressed; you get bitter. Life as you knew it is gone. All you can see is loss—and you're angry with God.

Now imagine the same situation—you just saw your house burn down. You've lost everything, all your valuables—your family treasures are nothing but smoking ash. But . . . you look next to you and see your family—all safe and alive. You realize you could have been in that house when it burned, but you weren't. You realize all you lost were things—and most could be replaced. And you experience thankfulness and gratitude to God for keeping you and your family safe through a terrible calamity.

Same experience, two starkly different reactions. Now let me ask you: Which reaction would you rather have? The second reaction is often what God gives to His children rather than protecting them from all loss and calamity. The Bible says that God causes it to rain on the just and the unjust alike (Matthew 5:45 NKJV). But to His children God gives grace through it. He guards our heart and soul, the most important things we have. Peace of heart and peace of mind are what we really want most. And God gives that to those who trust Him.

This is why I feel so sorry for people who have no Lord in heaven. When trouble hits and they are devastated, they can only look at the problem or inwardly at themselves. And there is no hope in either of those directions. As Christians we can turn our eyes away from the problem and onto the God who gives us grace and peace even in these times.

And we can look ahead of this dark, dark time in our lives and read the last chapter. We know how the story ends. We know how our story ends. And no chapter in our life, or series of chapters, can change that. David understood that.

For the LORD has heard the voice of my weeping. The LORD has
heard my supplication, the LORD receives my prayer. All my enemies
will be ashamed and greatly dismayed; they shall turn back, they will
suddenly be ashamed. (vv. 8–10)

David knows he will be saved because he's been saved before, and his enemies, who would like to celebrate over his defeat, will be shamed. He doesn't
know just how this is going to happen yet, but he knows it will. God has always
rescued him. Often when we are facing a great obstacle, if we are on the opti-
mistic side, like me, we can easily envision three or four scenarios where God
could rescue us. So we feel comfortable. We might even mistakenly call it faith.

But when God doesn't do any of those things, we can grow troubled. Now
our faith has to be stronger. But if you've walked with the Lord long enough, you
will have experienced His rescue, so you too can say, "The Lord has heard my
supplication, . . . the Lord receives my prayer. All my enemies will be ashamed;
. . . they shall turn back" (vv. 9–10). David is dismayed now, but he knows that
"all my enemies will be ashamed and greatly dismayed."

Though David has sinned in some way, and God has brought discipline
through his enemies, David also knows that his enemies will be dealt with by
God. They were planning evil against David, and God will cause that same evil
to fall on them.

When we sin and disobey God as Christians, God will bring discipline to
correct us. It won't be pleasant and might last longer than we'd like. But God
will eventually restore us if we repent before Him. If we, like David, reach for
the promise of grace, God will give it to us. And we will be able to move beyond
sin's discontents and into His presence and favor again.

Where Is Jesus in Psalm 6?

The terrible agony of fear and terror was also experienced by our Lord. In the
garden of Gethsemane, He literally sweat drops of blood. In medical terms,
He experienced *hematohidrosis*. It occurs in people suffering from extreme fear
or stress. Around the sweat glands there are multiple blood vessels in a netlike
form, which constrict under the pressure of great stress.

Does God really understand your suffering? Can He relate when you cry
out to Him how great your pain and stress are? Yes. He can. Imagine Jesus in the

garden of Gethsemane, and imagine Him quoting this psalm—and there you will see our Lord in Psalm 6. Every part of it fits Him—except that He wasn't suffering and agonizing for His own sin but for yours. He experienced sin and its discontents at a level so terrible that it overwhelmed the Son of God. Let that idea sink in.

You may be going through a season of sin and discontentment. It's tearing you apart, and it's not going to get any better until you turn away from the sin and back to God. He doesn't need to return to you—you need to return to Him. You moved; He didn't. Come back to Him today. Leave sin and you will leave its discontents behind as well.

Speak this psalm. Pray it to God. Become the "I" in this psalm. God is giving you powerful and poignant words to speak to Him.

Approach Him and . . . be honest.

QUESTIONS

1. Is there a fracture in your relationship with God over some issue? If so, how is it affecting your relationship and walk with Him? Have you ever had a fracture in your relationship with God? Do you remember how it felt?

2. As you have grown in your relationship with God, how has His presence in your life made you more aware of your own shortcomings? Why do you think this happens?

3. Try to think of a time when God dramatically answered your call for help in a way you could never have anticipated or expected. What did you learn of Him?

Chapter Four

The Question Everyone Wants to Ask God

Psalm 10

Deus absconditus. It's the Latin phrase meaning "the hidden God." Margaret Manning Shull writes,

> The hiddenness of God is a particularly painful experience for those who affirm faith in God. It is equally difficult for people who do not affirm any faith. *Where is this hidden God believers want us to follow? Why doesn't God show up?*

This is, as we will see, the question everyone wants to ask God. Shull then describes Jesus on the cross, alone and feeling abandoned. *Deus absconditus.*

> Perhaps, like Jesus, there are times when the best we can do is to yield ourselves to the God who seems hidden behind the clouds—and perhaps to acknowledge that the journey to faith is not always the warm assurance of perpetually clear skies that we thought it might

be. For those outside of faith, such admissions may well be a needed authenticity.

In this sense, as author Flannery O'Connor wrote, faith is not a guarantee of security and comfort: "I think there is no suffering greater than what is caused by the doubts of those who want to believe. I know what torment this is, but I can only see it, in myself anyways, as the process by which faith is deepened. . . . What people don't realize is how much religion costs. They think faith is like a big electric blanket, when of course it is a cross. . . . You arrive at enough certainty to be able to make your way, but it is making it in the darkness. . . . Faith . . . is trust, not certainty."[1]

In Psalm 10 we hear David's cry of lament, and in this cry he asks God three pertinent questions, the same questions we might be asking in our own lives. The same questions believers and nonbelievers alike have asked down through the centuries, beginning first with the most important and most powerful question.

Where Are You When I'm in Real Trouble?

When everything is going well, we are sure God is smiling down upon us and pouring out His blessings upon us. But when everything that can go wrong is going wrong, we ask a different question. Maybe we dare not even utter the words, but the thought is certainly on our mind. David was not afraid to ask:

Why do You stand afar off, O LORD? Why do You hide Yourself in times of trouble? (v. 1)

When we are going through severe trouble, especially at the hands of people who are cruel and heartless, one of our first reactions is confusion. "I'm a Christian! I honor and serve You, Lord. Why would You let this happen? When I pray and beg You to come and help, I get . . . nothing."

Radio silence.

"Where have You gone—especially now?" And maybe that's where you are right now. You are in real trouble and wondering how to apply your faith to this situation, or if you don't yet have faith in God, wondering if He's even there.

The human condition is that we live in a world filled with people who behave badly and make people's lives miserable. It's the reason some have walked away from their faith altogether. They trusted God to keep them safe—to always rescue them, keep them from danger—and when it became clear that God wasn't doing that, they felt He had been either negligent or impotent, and they walked away.

They will say, "I believed in God, I trusted God, and He didn't come through." Tim Keller frequently reminds us that if we leave God when He doesn't do what we expect Him to do, we're really only trusting Him to meet our own agenda. That's not biblical faith or trust. It's just a business transaction. "If you keep up Your end, God, by meeting all my expectations, I'll keep up my end and keep believing in You. What could be fairer than that?"

That's not worship—it's simply business, where God has to continually earn our trust to secure our patronage. So when we aren't seeing the results we expect or want, we say, "Why do you stand afar off, O LORD? Why do You hide Yourself in times of trouble?"

"Man, God, where are You?"

The Prayer of Loneliness (Disappointment)

It's easy to belittle people who have reacted this way, or claim they had no real faith to begin with. After all, we might think smugly, no one who truly trusted God would respond this way—they would only spout words of faith and trust. We feel certain this is the correct spiritual pose. But deep, deep down, if you believe in God, really believe in God, and are experiencing circumstances that threaten to overwhelm you—this is a truly honest and accepted prayer.

It is a good prayer. And it's not sinful.

Do you want me to prove that to you? Listen to Matthew 27:45–46. "Now from the sixth hour darkness fell upon all the land until the ninth hour. And about the ninth hour Jesus cried out with a loud voice, saying, 'Eli, Eli, lama sabachthani?' that is, 'My God, My God, why have You forsaken Me?'" Jesus, our Savior, prayed this prayer.

On the cross, Jesus, fully man, felt abandoned by God to His enemies. And in the greatest anguish yelled loudly, "God, why have You forsaken Me?" It was an honest cry—sharing the anguish He felt at the only separation from the Father He had experienced from all eternity. Jesus, in that moment, was quoting the psalm He knew so well, Psalm 22:1–2: "My God, my God, why have You forsaken me? Far from my deliverance are the words of my groaning. O my God, I cry by day, but You do not answer; and by night, but I have no rest."

Didn't Jesus know He would rise again after death? Yes! He prophesied of it numerous times (Matthew 12:38–40; 20:19; Luke 18:33). Did He trust His heavenly Father completely? Yes. No one has ever trusted the Father more perfectly. But as a man representing you and me, He was, for the moment, being forsaken by the Father. He felt abandoned because He was being abandoned to endure the suffering for sin we deserved. It was an honest cry of anguish. Jesus was literally shouting Scripture—Scripture that had deeper meaning to Him at that moment than we can possibly imagine.

Remember, the Psalms teach us how to talk to God in the hardest times of life—without sinning, that is, without offending God in the process. And yet even in this moment, it is not what it appears. Jesus is not disconnecting from God; He is connecting with God. He is going back to God's Word, the Scriptures. He was finding refuge and hope in the words of God. God's Word is true. The prophecies concerning it must be fulfilled.

There are times when God seems . . . so far away. It seems as if God is hiding from us. So we learn in the Psalms it's OK to express to God what you feel even if it's not ultimately what you believe. We can believe strongly that God will never forsake us—but there are times in life when God will allow us to feel as if He has. And He will allow us to say what we feel even when we know it's not the final truth.

Where Is God When It Hurts?

Author Philip Yancey, in a magazine article, recounted his experience when asked to speak at the memorial service after the Sandy Hook Elementary School shooting in Newtown, Connecticut. The community was reeling from the murder of twenty children and six teachers and staff just a few days earlier. He spoke about this question: Where is God when it hurts?

Deus absconditus.

But then he turned the question upside down.

In Newtown I asked the familiar question with a slight change:

Where is *no-God* when it hurts? The answer: As cosmic accidents, we live meaningless lives in a universe of random events and detached indifference. The parents who lost a child at Sandy Hook recoil from such a conclusion. Following the apostle Paul, most of them hold tightly to the hope that the existence of their son or daughter did not end on December 14, 2012; rather, a loving God will fulfill the promise to make all things new.

He wrote again,

Where is God when it hurts? My first answer centers on the holiday celebrated 11 days after Sandy Hook. For whatever reason, God has chosen to respond to our predicament not by waving a magic wand to make evil and suffering disappear, but by joining us and absorbing it in his very person.

In the Message, Eugene Peterson translates the familiar verse in John's prologue as, "The Word became flesh and blood, and moved into the neighborhood." What kind of neighborhood did Jesus move into? I asked the folks in Newtown. The Currier and Ives scene of pristine lawns and Victorian frame houses? Oh no—this neighborhood, as Matthew reminds us: "A voice is heard in Ramah . . . Rachel weeping for her children and refusing to be comforted, because they are no more." The Christmas story includes a setting much like . . . Newtown. Scholars tell us that the small town of Bethlehem likely had around 20—*20!*—children of the age that Herod slaughtered. In the end, God, "who did not spare his own Son, but gave him up for us all" (Rom. 8:32), lost a child too. [2]

David asks a question so many of us will ask. Where are You when I'm in real trouble? But then he continues with another powerful question . . .

Why Do You Let the Wicked Get Away with Murder?

David, like so many of us, is experiencing wicked people acting wickedly against him, and cries out honestly:

In pride the wicked hotly pursue the afflicted; let them be caught in the plots which they have devised. For the wicked boasts of his heart's desire, and the greedy man curses and spurns the LORD. The wicked, in the haughtiness of his countenance, does not seek Him. All his thoughts are, "There is no God." His ways prosper at all times; Your judgments are on high, out of his sight; as for all his adversaries, he snorts at them. He says to himself, "I will not be moved; throughout all generations I will not be in adversity." His mouth is full of curses and deceit and oppression; under his tongue is mischief and wicked-ness. He sits in the lurking places of the villages; in the hiding places he kills the innocent; his eyes stealthily watch for the unfortunate. He lurks in a hiding place as a lion in his lair; he lurks to catch the afflicted; he catches the afflicted when he draws him into his net. He crouches, he bows down, and the unfortunate fall by his mighty ones. He says to himself, "God has forgotten; He has hidden His face; He will never see it." (vv. 2–11)

Here is a lengthy description of the kind of people David is talking about and something learned from his own experience. The wicked are depicted as con-stantly chasing the afflicted. So David requests, "Let them be caught in the plots which they have devised" (v. 2).

A common theme in Psalms is that the wicked would be caught in their own traps. Whatever evil traps the wicked lay for others, may they get caught in them themselves. As Haman was hung on the stake he designed for righteous Mordecai in the book of Esther (Esther 7:9–10), as the Egyptian army was destroyed in the Red Sea—the place they planned to destroy the Hebrews—(Exodus 14), as Joseph was given power over his brothers who had sold him into slavery and tried to destroy him (Genesis 45), each guilty party was caught in the plots they had devised.

God does not mind this prayer. He has said that what a man sows, thus shall he reap (Galatians 6:7). I have found myself praying this prayer at times. I am only asking God to fulfill His divine law that He created our world with—what a man sows, he shall reap. Sow evil, reap evil. God does not mind us ask-ing that He hold people accountable for the evil they plan for others. After all, David points out, "the wicked hotly pursue the afflicted" (v. 2).

> God does not mind us asking that He hold people accountable for the evil they plan for others.

The wicked person is boastful and spurns and curses the Lord. He is proud and arrogant, and this is all because he "does not seek Him. All his thoughts are, 'There is no God'" (v. 4). His words are cruel and hurtful, full of deceit and malice. He's a jerk. And proud of it! He sees everyone else as a sucker or a target. He can arrive at this condition because he has convinced himself God does not exist.

It's logical. When a person jettisons the idea of God, and divine accountability for their actions, morality becomes relative. And a morality that is relative—meaning what's moral to you isn't necessarily moral for everyone—is another way of saying there simply is no objective morality, no real right or wrong. We can say there is a morality, but there is no objective basis for it—it's just what we happen to feel at the time.

And as we have seen in our own culture, when you jettison the idea of God from society, morality begins to be first questioned, then challenged, and finally abandoned. But notice something interesting in verse 4 and verse 11. In verse 4 we read, "The wicked, in the haughtiness of his countenance, does not seek Him. All his thoughts are, 'There is no God.'" But in verse 11 we read, "He says to himself, 'God has forgotten; He has hidden His face; He will never see it.'"

What we see in verse 4 is bravado—he doesn't want there to be a God; he doesn't want life to be like that. So he loudly proclaims what he *wants* to be true. He wants to create a new paradigm in which God is not real and he is not accountable to Him. But here is the problem: it's not easy to do that. We live in a world with incredible complexity of design.

Everyone Has Doubts

C. S. Lewis wrote about his own occasional doubts:

I think the trouble with me is *lack of faith*; I have no *rational* ground for going back on the arguments that convinced me of God's existence; but the irrational deadweight of my own skeptical habits, and the spirit of this age, and the cares of the day, steal away all my lively feeling of the truth; and often when I pray, I wonder if I am not posting letters to a non-existent address. Mind you, I don't think so—the whole of my reasonable mind is convinced: but I often feel so . . . But even atheists doubt![3]

In another place, Lewis wrote,

Just as the Christian has his moments when the clamor of this visible and audible world is so persistent, and the whisper of the spiritual world is so faint that faith and reason can hardly stick to their guns, so, as I well remember, the atheist has his moments of shuddering misgivings of an all but irresistible suspicion that old tales may, after all, be true, that something or someone from outside may at any moment break into his neat, explicable, mechanical universe. Believe in God, and you will have to face hours when it seems obvious that this material world is the only reality; disbelieve in Him, and you must face hours when this material world seems to shout at you that it is not all. No conviction, religion, or irreligion will, of itself, end once and for all this fifth columnist of the soul.[4]

In short, a person may be a practicing atheist or agnostic, if not always a convinced one. Regardless of what you believe, doubt will raise its head at times.

Then David continues, "His ways prosper at all times; Your judgments are on high, out of his sight" (v. 5). The point is that while they are actively engaged in evil, it looks as if everything is going their way.

Before Harvey Weinstein was arrested for sexually assaulting so many women, he was living the high life. Before Bill Cosby was arrested for sexually assaulting women, he was a Hollywood icon. Before Jeffrey Epstein was arrested and jailed, he was the man other men dreamed of being—wealthy beyond belief, able to indulge his every perverted desire, and seemingly untouchable. Each one of these men had been accused of illegal acts before but had been able to evade arrest and punishment. They got away with it and continued living the sinful life. It emboldened them. Such a man says to himself, "I will not be moved; Throughout all generations I will not be in adversity" (v. 6).

Recently another pastor fell into immorality. When it was exposed, it was found he had done this before, and the church knew about it. Sin, when it isn't judged immediately, emboldens you to keep going. No one considers a bigger step of sin unless they have gotten away with a smaller sin before. God has judged them already, but they can't see it yet. They are moving toward His judgment like a mouse bravely stalking cheese in a trap. They develop a false sense of security.

And David pictures the wicked as predators, lurking, hiding, stealthily stalking. They crouch; they trap. It's no surprise that such people in our own culture are labeled predators. A senior citizen scammed out of their savings by someone claiming to be an IRS agent; a poor family threatened with eviction by a wicked landlord if they report appliances that don't work, or broken windows, or rodents; a student who desperately needs a passing grade is told they will have to earn the grade through sex. It goes on and on.

To think, to even imagine that somehow they are going to get away with this is unimaginable. But at the moment, it sure seems like they are. And that leads to the final question.

When Are You Going to Put an End to It?

That is the final cry of someone who is being victimized. So David cries out,

> Arise, O LORD; O God, lift up Your hand. Do not forget the afflicted.
> Why has the wicked spurned God? He has said to himself, "You will
> not require it." You have seen it, for You have beheld mischief and
> vexation to take it into Your hand. The unfortunate commits himself
> to You; You have been the helper of the orphan. Break the arm of the
> wicked and the evildoer, seek out his wickedness until You find none.
>
> The LORD is King forever and ever; nations have perished from
> His land. O LORD, You have heard the desire of the humble; You
> will strengthen their heart, You will incline Your ear to vindicate the
> orphan and the oppressed, so that man who is of the earth will no
> longer cause terror. (vv. 12–18)

Like the sun on a cloudy day finally breaks through, so the psalmist's faith finally breaks through. Ironically, this last part of the passage shows us a man who never gets the *why* questions answered yet who trusts God completely because he has seen God deal with the righteous and the wicked in his past. He cries out, "Do not forget the afflicted" (v. 12).

Where Is Jesus in Psalm 10?

God did not forget the afflicted—He *joined* them.

Jesus left the glory of heaven and dove down into our world and entered our suffering. So we read in Isaiah 53:3–8 that Jesus would be "despised and forsaken . . . a man of sorrows and acquainted with grief . . . despised . . . stricken, smitten of God and afflicted . . . pierced through for our transgressions . . . crushed for our iniquities . . . [scourged] . . . oppressed and afflicted . . . taken away . . . cut off from the land of the living for the transgressions of my people, to whom the stroke was due." Evil, wicked men turned on their creator, and He allowed it—all because of His love for us. Jesus did not come to live the good life but to rescue us.

In the Old Testament the people of God could only ask the questions, depend on their experience with God in the past, trust in what God said, and hope in Him. But today, from our vantage point, we can see *how* God answered: Jesus came and entered our suffering.

He did not forget the afflicted.

David calls out for God to arise like a warrior and fight for the innocent, to act on their behalf. Why has the wicked spurned God? He has said to himself, "You will not require it" (v. 13). You have seen it, for You have beheld mischief and vexation to take it into Your hand. Only today do we see how carefully and wonderfully God took our rescue from evil into His hand, personally, through Jesus (1 Peter 3:18).

"You have been the helper of the orphan. Break the arm of the wicked and the evildoer, seek out his wickedness until You find none" (vv. 14–15). David remembers that God has protected the orphans, so he asks boldly for God to break the arm of the wicked. This was a symbolic way of asking God to break their power. Power was represented by a man's right hand, normally his most powerful (unless he was a lefty). And David asks God to so deal with the wicked that they can't do wickedness anymore. "Seek out his wickedness until You find none."

"The LORD is King forever and ever; nations have perished from His land" (v. 16). David reminds himself that the ultimate power in the universe is not the wicked but the Lord, the King, and that He has singlehandedly destroyed the power of nations. So David ends with "O LORD, You have heard the desire of the humble; You will strengthen their heart, You will incline Your ear to vindicate the orphan and the oppressed, so that man who is of the earth will no longer cause terror" (vv. 17–18). The humble are those who cannot protect themselves.

Faith counts on God to keep His word. He will encourage, with His presence, those being oppressed and will intervene at the proper time. And one day Jesus will perfectly fulfill this truth that "man who is of the earth will no longer cause terror." When Jesus comes again to judge the world, all wickedness and evil will be done away with forever. The man of Earth will no longer cause terror (Matthew 25:31–46; Revelation 21:5–8).

Maybe this is where you are today. You have been, in some way, victimized. Some person or group has done evil to you, and it seems as if they have gotten away with it. That thought is tearing you up. The idea that they will never have to answer for it is stealing your happiness, draining your joy. Today, God wants you to give that over to Him.

He is the judge—let Him carry that burden of judgment. He wants you to know He will deal specifically with the evil they have done to you. Let that thought strengthen your heart. Let go of your need to administer justice—God sees, and He will judge.

This does not mean if you are currently being abused that you are to stay and endure it—you should seek every legal means to stay safe—but let the desire for revenge go. God's got this. He'll handle it. Let it go.

Three questions we all ask: Where are you when I'm in real trouble? Why do you let the wicked get away with murder? When are you going to put an end to it? The answers are that He is always with us, no one is getting away with anything, and one day God will deal fully with all the evil that has ever been done, and specifically to you.

Jesus has experienced all these things. He was in real trouble. He was even murdered though He was innocent, but though He was crucified, God raised Him from the dead. We worship a suffering Savior, one who has experienced all the pains of life that we have so that He could bring us salvation, rescue. And for our sakes He dealt fully with the evil that we had done against God and one another on the cross.

Whether or not you feel like you are in real trouble, if you don't know Christ as your Savior, you are. Your sins are still judging you. They still alienate you from Him. Though He is a loving God, He is also a holy God. But the gospel (good news) is that He has already judged your sins in Christ, so He can freely offer you forgiveness and peace with Him if you will simply put your faith in what Jesus did for you on the cross.

Deus absconditus, the hidden God, is hidden no more. He has come. Will you receive His mercy and grace?

QUESTIONS

1. Have you ever gone through a period of doubt in God when you desperately wanted to believe? What was (is) it that was causing your doubt? What belief about God were your emotions struggling with?

2. The Psalms seem to teach clearly that it is OK to express what you feel to God, even if it's not ultimately what you believe. Have you ever felt the freedom to do that?

3. There are times when we are truly treated evilly by people. What does this psalm, and other psalms, teach us are valid prayers to pray regarding the wicked (see v. 2)? Have you ever dared to pray such a prayer? How do we balance a sinful desire for vengeance with a righteous desire for justice?

Chapter Five

Joy Comes in the Morning

Psalm 30

Joni Eareckson Tada had a diving accident at the age of seventeen and became a quadriplegic. It changed her life dramatically, but not in the way you might think. God changed her life for the better, not the worse. A few years ago she wrote an article, "Reflections on the 50th Anniversary of My Diving Accident." What does she think about life and God after all that?

She wrote,

> What a difference time makes—as well as prayer, heaven-minded friends, and a deep study of God's Word. All combined, I began to see there *are* more important things in life than walking and having use of your hands. It sounds incredible, but I really would rather be in this wheelchair knowing Jesus as I do than be on my feet without him.

She talks later about the process.

The process is difficult, but affliction isn't a killjoy; I don't think you could find a happier follower of Jesus than me. The more my paralysis helps me get disentangled from sin, the more joy bubbles up from within. I can't tell you how many nights I have lain in bed, unable to move, stiff with pain, and have whispered near tears, "Oh, Jesus, I'm so happy. So very happy in you!" . . .

Grace softens the edges of past pains, helping to highlight the eternal. What you are left with is peace that's profound, joy that's unshakable, faith that's ironclad.[1]

Psalm 30 echoes the experience of Joni and so many others who have walked with God. It gives thanks for what God has done over the long haul of life in spite of the pain and suffering. It reminds us that joy comes in the morning! David is going to show us that joy comes first of all . . .

When We Remember How God Rescued Us

Suffering and pain are so hard to go through, especially if they arrive because of behavior and decisions we have made, and yet later, when we see what God has done in our lives through these, we can look at them so differently. So David writes,

Thanksgiving for Deliverance from Death. A Psalm; a Song at the Dedication of the House. A Psalm of David.

I will extol You, O LORD, for You have lifted me up, and have not let my enemies rejoice over me. O LORD my God, I cried to You for help, and You healed me. O LORD, You have brought up my soul from Sheol; You have kept me alive, that I would not go down to the pit. Sing praise to the LORD, you His godly ones, And give thanks to His holy name. For His anger is but for a moment, His favor is for a lifetime; weeping may last for the night, but a shout of joy comes in the morning. (vv. 1–5)

This psalm, David tells us, is a song of dedication of the house. Some schol-ars believe David wrote this psalm after his own home was built, and it caused him to look back over his life. He was able to look at what God had done in his life, to see how God had taken him from a shepherd in the field to the king of a mighty nation. Shepherds didn't have any upward mobility normally, so David was in awe of God.

David sees God's hand in so much of his life, even in the pain and suffering he had to go through. Tim Keller wrote, "This is a song of grace. While God can be angry with His people, anger is never the final word, and so joy is always on the way, always coming to those who believe in Him." [2] Every Christian who has walked with God enough years can relate to this.

David says, "I will extol You, O LORD, for You have lifted me up" (v. 1). The word in Hebrew translated "lifted me up" is the word used for pulling up a bucket from a well. David likens his situation to being in a deep hole he can't get out of. In verse 3 we see how deep that well was in his mind. "You have brought up my soul from Sheol; You have kept me alive, that I would not go down to the pit."

David was in danger of death, from either sickness or enemies. His concern is that "my enemies rejoice over me" (v. 1). David's concern was that his enemies would conclude by his death that God could not, or would not, deliver him. Whatever the danger was, it was real. But David cried out to God and God rescued him.

We often hear the phrase "there are no atheists in foxholes," meaning that when someone faces a danger they can't handle, and nothing else can save them, they are tempted to throw up a prayer to a God they don't really believe in. But even if they send up the prayer, there is no faith in it—it's only desperation.

And if God saves them, they won't give a thought to God again. They'll forget all about their prayer and attribute their rescue to some other means—fate, luck, destiny. The great danger only reminded them that there are times when we are truly helpless and cannot save ourselves, and they don't like that feeling. That is the idea they are rejecting.

God, in His mercy, reminds them of their need for Him through a circumstance they can't control. When they call out to Him, and He indeed rescues them, they promptly forget all about it and act again as if God did not exist. But the child of God does not do that. We remember what we asked God to do, and we celebrate His rescue of us.

See something important here though. David wants the community of believers to join in praise for what God has done in his life. When God rescues us, delivers us, provides for us, protects us, we are not to keep it a secret: "Sing praise to the LORD, you His godly ones, and give thanks to His holy name" (v. 4).

The Need for Public Praise

Don't you get excited when you hear how God has helped someone, healed someone, provided for someone, protected someone—especially if you need God to do that for you? Who do you tell when God answers an important prayer request? Who knows how God is working in your life? Who knows what you are praising God for? Who are you enlisting to pray and praise with you? "Sing praise to the LORD, you His godly ones, and give thanks to His holy name."

It would not do the church a bit of harm if some of us began to write out psalms of thanksgiving to our God, speaking of what He has done in our lives! What prompts David's outburst of praise? This one powerful truth: "For His anger is but for a moment, His favor is for a lifetime; weeping may last for the night, but a shout of joy comes in the morning" (v. 5).

There are people convinced that they got on the wrong side of God once and will be there forever. They made God so mad, or did something so bad, He can never forgive them. We think that because we have experienced that in life: we have offended someone so bad they won't ever talk to us again or forgive us. We project that onto God. But it doesn't fit God.

When God hides His face from His children, it is to cause them to come running back to Him. He always wants to reconcile with you. That sin that you feel you can never overcome, He did. What you did was bad and did indeed deserve God's punishment—so He punished it. But instead of giving you what you really deserve, He took the punishment Himself, satisfying both His justice and His holiness.

As Paul wrote to the Corinthian church, "He made Him who knew no sin to be sin on our behalf, so that we may become the righteousness of God in Him" (2 Corinthians 5:21). God doesn't just forgive us—He gives us the righteousness of His Son, Jesus. It's why Paul said right before this, "Therefore, we are ambassadors for Christ, as though God were making an appeal through us; we beg you on behalf of Christ, be reconciled to God" (v. 20).

"His anger is but for a moment, His favor is for a lifetime; weeping may last for the night, but a shout of joy comes in the morning." God's full anger against your sin was poured out in full on Christ on the cross. Three days later Jesus triumphed over the grave.

"A shout of joy comes in the morning!"

Joy comes when we remember how God rescued us. Can you remember the times God rescued you? Have you written them down, to make an Ebenezer, a reminder of God's faithfulness to you? Perhaps you should. We can still write psalms today! But David goes on: "joy comes in the morning" when . . .

We Remember How We Failed Him

Yes, even our failures call for praise, because God rescued us from our failings and failures as well. So David writes,

> Now as for me, I said in my prosperity, "I will never be moved." O Lord, by Your favor You have made my mountain to stand strong; You hid Your face, I was dismayed. To You, O Lord, I called, and to the Lord I made supplication: "What profit is there in my blood, if I go down to the pit? Will the dust praise You? Will it declare Your faithfulness?" (vv. 6–9)

There are times when we can feel "I have arrived!" All that we were seeking we have achieved. I remember a time like that in my own life. I was a young church planter, and I was standing on the front lawn of my new house in Rancho Santa Margarita. I was remembering how I had struggled for so many years to complete my education, skimping and clawing to meet just my basic needs. I was lonely, had no time to date, no social life, and was renting a one-bedroom apartment and barely making the rent month to month. My paperhanging business was not always paying the bills. I was frequently overwhelmed and exhausted.

All that time I dreamed of the day when I would be a paid pastor working full time in God's ministry, giving myself entirely to God's Word. No more classes, no more hanging wallpaper, no more living month to month. Then in a period of just a few years, God answered all my prayers so powerfully. I met

Annette, we got married, I got my degree, we had two kids, I got a full-time job as a church planter, and we even bought a house in a brand-new community. We had even bought a brand-new minivan. Man, I had arrived!

Everything I had wanted and dreamed of I had received. And I felt . . . proud. I thought of how hard I had worked, how much I had sacrificed, and how this was the payoff. "See," I told myself, "this is what happens when you work hard and apply yourself." I had every intention of setting up camp and staying in that mood and condition forever. "I said in my prosperity, I will never be moved" (v. 6).

David went on: "O LORD, by Your favor You have made my mountain to stand strong" (v. 7). "Mountain" was a symbol for all David's position and power and provision. He recognizes later where his blessings had really come from. So did I. And then I experienced what David and many believers have. "You hid Your face, I was dismayed" (v. 7).

A few short years later it was all threatening to come undone in my life. The church was divided, finances were tight, people were saying bad things about me, and I was sure I was going to have to quit. I would lose my job, my status, my home, my financial security.

Turns out I could be moved after all.

I needed to learn that what I had received, though I had indeed worked hard, was because of grace. Many worked far harder than me, and were more gifted than me, but hadn't had the unique opportunities God had given me.

So like David, the only time I really appreciated what I had been given was when it was almost taken from me. "I was dismayed." But in that horrible moment I turned to God and to the "LORD I called, and to the Lord I made supplication" (v. 8). And I learned again that "His anger is for a moment. . . . His favor is for a lifetime" (v. 5).

Turtles on a Fence Post

We forget that it is from God's hands that we have what we have. We forget that we are all turtles on a fence post. The story has been frequently told that if you see a turtle straddled on a fence post, one thing you can be sure is that it didn't get there by itself. Turtles can't climb fences. Someone put it there. We are all turtles on a fence.

I love to read success stories of people who are trying to explain their success to others. They speak of how hard they worked, how they sacrificed, pulled themselves up by their bootstraps, overcame doubters. But only occasionally do you come across truly honest and humble people who can admit the truth—it was a fortunate break or series of breaks that led to their success.

J. K. Rowling, author of the Harry Potter books and possibly the most successful author of our time, had submitted her book through an agent to many publishers who all rejected it and even told her she couldn't write for children. Finally, over a year later, the chairman of a publishing house wasn't very excited about the proposal, but on a lark he gave it to his young daughter. She read it and loved it . . . and the rest is history. Rowling realized how important that moment was to her ultimate success. [3]

A man named Theodore Geisel was walking down a street dejectedly one afternoon, carrying a children's book he had written. It had been rejected by twenty-seven publishers. He was going to throw it away. On the way he happened upon an old friend who greeted him and saw he was rather dejected. He asked him what was wrong, and Geisel said he had written a children's book no one wanted and was going to go throw it away. His friend, however, just happened to be a newly minted editor at a book house—the children's book editor, in fact. And the rest is history. *On Mulberry Street* by Dr. Seuss became history. Dr. Seuss once said that had he been walking on the other side of the street, it was likely he would never have become a children's author. [4]

This helps make sense of David's words: "You have made my mountain to stand strong; You hid Your face, I was dismayed" (v. 7). God blesses, and He can withdraw blessings. He makes us stand strong, and He can hide His face. Not recognizing God's movement in your life can be tragic. We are not independent contractors. There is a God. So David continued: "To You, O LORD, I called, and to the Lord I made supplication: 'What profit is there in my blood, if I go down to the pit? Will the dust praise You? Will it declare Your faithfulness?'" (vv. 8–9).

David is saying to God, "What will it profit you, Lord, if I die and my life can no longer give you praise and honor and glory?" He knows we were made to give God glory—that is the reason for our creation.

You weren't primarily created to be of value to others—you were created to glorify God. And there will never be a time when you can't do that. You are not a commodity whose value goes up or down based on your age and usefulness.

Your purpose at fifteen, at fifty, and at one hundred years of age is precisely the same. You are to glorify God with your heart, soul, mind, and body.

David sees the joy coming to him when he remembers this even when he failed God. Yet finally David sees his joy coming when . . .

We Remember How He Turned Our Tears into Laughter

Each of us has had our share of tears, sadness, failure, and depression. But in Christ we can experience, even in the midst of that, and especially when God delivers us again, how He can turn our tears into laughter. So David writes,

"Hear, O Lord, and be gracious to me; O Lord, be my helper." You have turned for me my mourning into dancing; You have loosed my sackcloth and girded me with gladness, that my soul may sing praise to You and not be silent. O Lord my God, I will give thanks to You forever. (vv. 10–12)

David still needs God's favor and grace; he has learned that. He has learned that God must always be His help and His hope. But fortunately, now he has so many wonderful life experiences behind him to buttress that truth in his life. "You have turned for me my mourning into dancing; You have loosed my sackcloth and girded me with gladness, that my soul may sing praise to You and not be silent. O Lord my God, I will give thanks to You forever" (vv. 11–12).

Sackcloth was what you wore when you were in mourning and despair. It was an outward sign of your inward condition. This pictures God taking off David's sackcloth and putting on new clothes of gladness. David is remembering what God has done for him. It's a powerful memory because it reveals to him God's pattern of conduct in his life. God always helps, always forgives, always rescues when we call to Him.

God always helps, always forgives, always rescues when we call to Him.

When the prodigal son, in Luke 15:19–24, had finally made his way home after his journey away from his father and wisdom, he wondered how he would be received. He had been such a failure as a son. But what response did the father have? The father clothes his son with the robe of honor, puts his ring of authority upon his finger, puts sandals on his feet, and brings the fatted calf to feast on and celebrate his return. And this is a picture of how God awaits us and wants to turn our mourning into dancing, to loosen our sackcloth and gird us with happiness.

David does not say "my mouth" sings praise but "my soul." Our soul is the deepest part of us, the part that weeps before tears are formed, that rejoices before the smile even hits our face. It is the subterranean part of our heart where joy and sorrow are birthed. David wants the deepest part of his heart and soul to sing silently to God in praise—to be so overwhelmed with gladness that he can't stop it.

Tune Our Hearts to Sing Your Praise

How frequently we sit in a church service and sing worship songs—wonderful hymns and choruses of praise to God. We sing loudly and maybe even beautifully. But the words of praise come from our mouths, not as often from our hearts. Our minds and hearts are often a million miles away when we are singing. As God says in Isaiah, "This people draw near with their words and honor Me with their lip service, but they remove their hearts far from Me" (Isaiah 29:13).

True praise and worship are always the result of something God has done for us. If you want to truly worship God on your own or in a service, come before Him first with a sacrifice of praise. Remember what He has done for you and who He is, and let your soul engage in worship before you sing one word. Try preparing yourself for worship that way, and it will revolutionize worship for you. We truly need to tune our hearts to sing God's praise.

A lady at my first church sang solos. She had a pleasant voice, but in truth she went flat once in a while. But no one ever complained. The reason is that as she sang praises to God, tears were streaming down her face. Sometimes her voice choked up. We all knew her and knew that she loved Jesus that much. What she was singing was straight from her heart. We were seeing real worship. She was making an offering to her God.

Unlike Scrooge in *A Christmas Carol*, David, when he has been restored, doesn't promise to be a much better man. Instead, he promises to praise God and give Him thanks forever. David knows why he has been left on planet Earth. Do you?

Do you know why you are still here? There are many good things to do here on planet Earth that please God, and we should do those things. But that isn't why we were made. We were made to glorify God. He is the eternal sun, and we are all tiny moons designed to reflect His glory.

Any Christian at any age, and any stage of usefulness, still has that calling. Point people to God's goodness, His grace in Christ, His work in your life, and His mercies you have experienced. And at the end, your reward will be an eternal joy in an eternal morning.

Joy comes in the morning when we remember how God rescued us, how we failed Him, and yet how He then turned our tears into laughter.

Where Is Jesus in Psalm 30?

God lifted Him up as He lifted David up. God did not let Jesus's enemies rejoice over Him. Jesus cried out to God for help, and God helped Him. God brought Jesus's soul up from Sheol and kept Him alive so that He could not go down to the pit forever. Jesus's life, death, and resurrection are all reflected in Psalm 30.

God rescued His Son, as Jesus took our failings to the cross and there turned our tears into laughter. Joy comes in the morning. You have failed God, but God wants to rescue you still. You can't see a reason to have any hope, yet God desires to give you that hope. But it is in Jesus, not in this life and its circumstances. All those can change and do change continually. What He has done for us, and who He is for us, never changes.

If you want the joy that comes in the morning, you need to come to Jesus.

Have you remembered how God rescued you? Do you tell Him your thanks? Do you remember how you have failed Him? Have you honestly confessed your shortcomings to Him? And when He turned your tears into laughter, did you praise Him? This is how God wants us to speak to Him and what He wants us to talk to Him about.

QUESTIONS

1. How has God reminded you of your need of Him through a circumstance you couldn't control? What have you learned that you didn't know before, and how has it changed you?

2. Take a moment and think of three to four times when God rescued you in a wonderful and amazing way and how it affected you. Write those down for your own memory. What was your shout of joy in the morning?

3. God not only blesses us but He also withdraws blessings from us for His purposes. He "makes [our] mountain to stand strong" but also "hides His face" from us. Have you experienced God withdrawing a blessing from you? What did it teach you about yourself and about God?

4. Write out a psalm of your own to God. Include both your desires and hopes as well as your thanks and praise for His work in your life. Share this psalm with others. (I did this with folks in our church after I finished this series, and we received so many beautiful psalms. Everyone was moved by this experience.)

Chapter Six

Seeking Vindication: Learning to Pray through the Unfairness of Life

Psalm 35

As much as we would wish it otherwise, life is frequently unfair. And occasionally it is dangerously, evilly unfair. We have been attacked, violated, humiliated by those we trusted and even befriended. How should we respond to that?

Rachael Denhollander was a US Olympic gymnast, and like so many other female gymnasts, she had been sexually molested by Larry Nasser, the former Team USA gymnastics doctor. In January 2018 she was given forty minutes to address the court—and her convicted abuser—during his sentencing. She said,

> You have become a man ruled by selfish and perverted desires, a man defined by his daily choices over and over again to feed that selfishness and perversion. You chose to pursue your wickedness no matter what it cost others.

She then referenced a Bible he had brought to court:

> The Bible you speak carries a final judgment where all of God's wrath and eternal terror is poured out on men like you. Should you ever reach the point of truly facing what you have done, the guilt will be crushing. . . .
>
> I pray you experience the soul-crushing weight of guilt so that you may someday experience true repentance and true forgiveness from God, which you need far more than forgiveness from me . . . though I extend that to you as well. . . .
>
> Larry, I can call what you did evil and wicked because it was. And I know it was evil and wicked because the straight line exists. The straight line is not measured based on your perception, or anyone else's perception, and this means I can speak the truth about my abuse without minimization or mitigation. And I can call it evil because I know what goodness is. And this is why I pity you. Because when a person loses the ability to define good and evil, when they cannot define evil, they can no longer define and enjoy what is truly good.[1]

Rachael was sinned against horribly, and she was innocent. She had never done anything to deserve her abuse. But her faith in God allowed her to respond with grace and truth, and at the end to be vindicated and blessed—and to bless and honor God in the process.

Psalm 35 is a prayer for vindication. David needed vindication, and he was praying for it. He had been unjustly abused, and it was continuing. Maybe you are struggling with an evil someone has done to you or is doing to you. How do you respond? How do you pray? Psalm 35 gives us that direction. David asks God three things. The first thing is to . . .

Fight the Battles I Can't Fight

A phrase often thrown around by people is "I don't need anyone to fight my battles for me." It's a statement of pride and bravado. Yet here we see David—soldier, warrior, general, giant slayer—disagreeing. David begins this psalm asking God to fight for him:

Contend, O LORD, with those who contend with me; fight against those who fight against me. Take hold of buckler and shield and rise up for my help. Draw also the spear and the battle-axe to meet those who pursue me; say to my soul, "I am your salvation." Let those be ashamed and dishonored who seek my life; let those be turned back and humiliated who devise evil against me. Let them be like chaff before the wind, with the angel of the LORD driving them on. Let their way be dark and slippery, with the angel of the LORD pursuing them. For without cause they hid their net for me; without cause they dug a pit for my soul. Let destruction come upon him unawares, and let the net which he hid catch himself; into that very destruction let him fall.

And my soul shall rejoice in the LORD; it shall exult in His salvation. All my bones will say, "LORD, who is like You, who delivers the afflicted from him who is too strong for him, and the afflicted and the needy from him who robs him?" (vv. 1–10)

"Contend, O LORD, with those who contend with me; fight against those who fight against me" (v. 1). It's a rather strange way to begin a hymn, isn't it? But David was being bullied, and he was asking God to not only get in the fight but take it over for him. Picture a tag-team wrestling match on TV, where one wrestler is in the match with two other wrestlers and is being overwhelmed. He has only enough energy to reach out his hand to his partner, waiting to enter and come to his rescue.

That's the type of scene David is describing. He is in grave danger and realizes he's overmatched and desperately needs to rest and let God take over the fight. It is thought by a number of scholars that this psalm refers to the time in David's life when he was not yet king, and King Saul of Israel was jealous of him and trying to assassinate him. First and foremost, this psalm is a prayer—a request for help.

David uses military language to ask God to go to war for him. "Take hold of buckler and shield and rise up for my help. Draw also the spear and the battle-axe to meet those who pursue me" (vv. 2–3). We might ask God to go to war by our side. "I'm being attacked, and I need you, Lord, to come and win the battle I am losing." Then David writes, "Say to my soul, 'I am your salvation'" (v. 3).

There are times in life when God is working to deliver us, but we can't see it. In fact, our deliverance may be right around the corner, but it *feels* as if it will never come. David is asking God to reassure him in his heart and for faith that He will, indeed, rescue him.

We can know in our heads that God will surely rescue us in some way—but what we desperately need is to *feel* safe in the midst of the danger. In that place within us where our fears live, we need to know *and feel* God will rescue us. David is asking God to bring him a deep assurance in his heart and faith that He will save him. Did you ever think it was OK to ask God for a feeling?

God wants us to know that He is our Savior. And not solely by what He did on the cross, but every day in every danger or fear we face. We all need a 24-7 Savior—and that's what He is, if we call on Him. Do you? Are you in trouble, danger, deep water, and unable to rescue yourself? Have you called out to God, or just to everyone and everything else? You may need to pray today, "Lord, say to my soul, 'I am your salvation.'"

Each person will one day be a victim of a particularly evil activity. You probably already have. I have on a number of occasions. But how does our faith help us? How does our faith make a difference?

If there is no God—and you have been falsely accused and cannot defend yourself, or undo what has been done—your only hope is to try to forget it and move on with your life. But that is a tall order. Someone you trusted violated your trust, and it significantly affected your life.

You've been hurt, violated. And what is worse, there is no punishment for your violator. They seemed to have gotten away with it. Sadly, they frequently do. You are angry and hurt and risk becoming bitter. That bitterness doesn't just affect you either—it affects all those who love you. This is all true . . . if there is no God, no final accounting.

A very familiar but anonymous quote is, "If you don't heal from what hurt you, you'll bleed on those who didn't cut you." People who never offended you, who in fact want only to be your friend, will have to bear the consequences of your still simmering bitterness.

What is the answer? Our faith tells us that God *has* seen it. And He *will* deal with it. That person will not get away with it. In fact, the punishment God will bring will be severe. What does David foresee for his enemies? "Let those be ashamed and dishonored who seek my life; let those be turned back and humiliated who devise evil against me. Let them be like chaff before the wind, with the angel of the LORD driving them on. Let their way be dark and slippery, with the angel of the LORD pursuing them" (vv. 4–6).

Poetic Justice

David foresees them being ashamed and dishonored by God as they shamed and dishonored David. Their evil plans will be ultimately thwarted. They will be like the chaff that blows away in the wind, never to return. And what is worse, it will be the angel of the Lord driving them into misery and dread. They won't be able to find their footing in life again, because the angel of the Lord (often the Lord Himself in the Old Testament) is making it happen. God will act. David is asking Him to do just that.

In fact, David goes further and asks for poetic justice. "Let destruction come upon him unawares, and let the net which he hid catch himself; into that very destruction let him fall" (v. 8). The evil man has set a trap for the good person—and wouldn't it be truly just if the evil person stumbled into his own trap?

A person who falsely calls someone a hypocrite is exposed as being a hypocrite himself. The criminal who parks in a neighborhood seeking to rob people, returns to find his car has been stolen. The person who pats themselves on the back for committing adultery and not getting caught, discovers their own spouse has committed adultery against them—and they hadn't known it. Poetic justice!

David is dealing with what everyone has to face sometime—unfair treatment. "For without cause they hid their net for me; without cause they dug a pit for my soul" (v. 7). David isn't asking God for vengeance—he is asking God for justice. He's crying out, "I didn't deserve this! They are attacking me for no good reason!" It's the same complaint Jesus echoed in John 15:25. Jesus knew that so many men in powerful places literally hated Him. So Jesus said in John 15:18, "If the world hates you, you know that it has hated Me before it hated you." In verse 23 Jesus said, "He who hates Me hates My Father also." Finally, Jesus quoted Psalm 35:7 when He said, "But they have done this to fulfill the word that is written in their Law, 'they hated Me without a cause'" (v. 25). Again, Jesus in the Psalms!

Peter the apostle reminds us that suffering unjustly, and not seeking vengeance, obtains favor with God:

> For this finds favor, if for the sake of conscience toward God a person bears up under sorrows when suffering unjustly. For what credit is there if, when you sin and are harshly treated, you endure it with patience? But if when you do what is right and suffer for it you patiently endure it, this finds favor with God.

For you have been called for this purpose, since Christ also suffered for you, leaving you an example for you to follow in His steps, who committed no sin, nor was any deceit found in His mouth; and while being reviled, He did not revile in return; while suffering, He uttered no threats, but kept entrusting Himself to Him who judges righteously. (1 Peter 2:19–23)

Now someone may say, "That idea of asking God to bring destruction to his enemies doesn't seem to be very New Testament, very gospel!" But it's not the destruction of his enemies that is the goal; it's deliverance from his enemies. David writes,

And my soul shall rejoice in the LORD; it shall exult in His salvation. All my bones will say, "LORD, who is like You, who delivers the afflicted from him who is too strong for him, and the afflicted and the needy from him who robs him?" (vv. 9–10)

There are simply times when the only way we can be delivered is if the evil are destroyed. If a man is trying to break into your home with a weapon and you call the police and they come, and in order to rescue you they shoot and kill the intruder, that wasn't your desire. You didn't even know the person—you had nothing against him. He was simply intent on doing you harm. The only way you could be delivered from danger was for him to be stopped, but his death or injury was not your primary goal. You just wanted to be rescued. That's all David is saying. It is not a contradiction of the gospel message.

Tim Keller in his devotional book on the Psalms, *The Songs of Jesus*, wrote a prayer that is appropriate for us all: "Lord, what others think of me is far too important to my heart. At times when I am being criticized unfairly, I need you to send your Spirit and speak to my soul, saying, 'I am your salvation—nothing else and no one else is.' Amen!"[2]

Lord, fight the battles I can't fight.

The first prayer seeking vindication is: Lord, fight the battles I can't fight. The next prayer is . . .

Deal with the Unfairness I Don't Deserve

It's bad enough when you are attacked, but it's beyond brutal when the ones attacking you are people you love and respect and had thought were really your friends. So David writes,

> Malicious witnesses rise up; they ask me of things that I do not know. They repay me evil for good, to the bereavement of my soul. But as for me, when they were sick, my clothing was sackcloth; I humbled my soul with fasting, and my prayer kept returning to my bosom. I went about as though it were my friend or brother; I bowed down mourning, as one who sorrows for a mother. But at my stumbling they rejoiced and gathered themselves together; the smiters whom I did not know gathered together against me, they slandered me without ceasing. Like godless jesters at a feast, they gnashed at me with their teeth.
>
> Lord, how long will You look on? Rescue my soul from their ravages, my only life from the lions. I will give You thanks in the great congregation; I will praise You among a mighty throng. (vv. 11–18)

David was being falsely accused of something, so he was being asked questions he could not answer because the accusations were false to begin with. It would be like someone accusing you of committing a crime you didn't commit—and then pressing you to give the details of how you did it. You could never satisfy them about how you did it because you hadn't committed the crime.

When we read this passage, we can't help but think of Jesus standing before the Sanhedrin in Matthew 26:59–60: "Now the chief priests and the whole Council kept trying to obtain false testimony against Jesus, so that they might put Him to death. They did not find any, even though many false witnesses came forward." At the trial of Stephen we read, "Then they secretly induced men to say, 'We have heard him speak blasphemous words against Moses and against God.' . . . They put forward false witnesses who said, 'This man incessantly speaks against this holy place and the law'" (Acts 6:11, 13). At Paul's trial before Festus we read, "The Jews . . . [brought] many and serious charges against him which they could not prove" (Acts 25:7). Lies are so powerful and effective. Satan uses them constantly.

What is so crushing to David is that these men who were lying about him, he had treated with kindness and goodness. "They repay me evil for good, to the bereavement of my soul. But as for me, when they were sick, my clothing was sackcloth; I humbled my soul with fasting, and my prayer kept returning to my bosom. I went about as though it were my friend or brother; I bowed down mourning, as one who sorrows for a mother" (vv. 12–13).

He had grieved when affliction had come upon these men, yet now that he was being afflicted, he says, "But at my stumbling they rejoiced and gathered themselves together; the smiters whom I did not know gathered together against me, they slandered me without ceasing. Like godless jesters at a feast, they gnashed at me with their teeth" (vv. 15–16). David isn't just being attacked but is also being betrayed. It's a powerful feeling.

Friendly Fire

When I was a young man at a church, a friend I had respected, looked up to, and admired wrote a letter to the elders about me filled with lies. I was beyond surprised. The things he said were easily disproven. It was clear he had gotten bad information somewhere, but what knocked the wind out of me was that it came from him. He had thought those things were true. When I tried to sit down and talk with him about it, he wouldn't do it. He didn't mind attacking me but didn't want to talk about it with me.

If someone has not maliciously accused you of doing something you haven't done, either (1) you haven't lived long enough, (2) you are leading a charmed life, or (3) your time is coming. It will happen. As a Christian, you should expect it from those who hate your Lord. But as a Christian, you can even be the victim of friendly fire from those who should be your brothers and sisters in Christ. Those wounds are more painful.

David is asking God to deal with the unfairness he is facing. "Lord, how long will You look on? Rescue my soul from their ravages, my only life from the lions. I will give You thanks in the great congregation; I will praise You among a mighty throng" (vv. 17–18). David is frustrated at how long God is allowing this to go on, a feeling many of us can identify with. But he also promises to praise God in the congregation when he is delivered.

David's last prayer is . . .

Vindicate Me So I Can Publicly Praise You

David wants his life and testimony to give praise and honor to God. So he asks God to work in such a way that he can do this with a wonderful testimony of God's faithfulness:

> Do not let those who are wrongfully my enemies rejoice over me; nor let those who hate me without cause wink maliciously. For they do not speak peace, but they devise deceitful words against those who are quiet in the land. They opened their mouth wide against me; they said, "Aha, aha, our eyes have seen it!"
>
> You have seen it, O LORD, do not keep silent; O Lord, do not be far from me. Stir up Yourself, and awake to my right and to my cause, my God and my Lord. Judge me, O LORD my God, according to Your righteousness, and do not let them rejoice over me. Do not let them say in their heart, "Aha, our desire!" Do not let them say, "We have swallowed him up!" Let those be ashamed and humiliated altogether who rejoice at my distress; let those be clothed with shame and dishonor who magnify themselves over me.
>
> Let them shout for joy and rejoice, who favor my vindication; and let them say continually, "The LORD be magnified, who delights in the prosperity of His servant." And my tongue shall declare Your righteousness and Your praise all day long. (vv. 19–28)

David is, in essence, turning judgment over to God here. David isn't saying, "This is what I'm going to do"—rather, he asks God to do this for him. "Do not let those who are wrongfully my enemies rejoice over me; nor let those who hate me without cause wink maliciously" (v. 19). It was hatred without cause. While this experience was a small part of David's life, it was what *defined* the life of our Lord.

So when you are feeling sorry for yourself because someone has hated you without cause—and treated you dreadfully—you are experiencing what David did for a season, and what our Lord experienced His whole earthly life. Remember that before you start getting mad at God for allowing it in your life. David is saying, "Don't let them say, 'We got everything we wanted—we have destroyed David—and David's God couldn't stop it!'" Don't let evil win!

The Spiritual Firewall

One of the realities the evil persons have to deal with is that they will never get all they want. They will be frustratingly unsatisfied in their evil pursuits because there is a hidden spiritual firewall that they can't breach around God's people. God allows them to go so far, but no further. They can harm, but they can't destroy. And it frustrates them. They want to rejoice over the godly man or woman's destruction, but ultimately God denies them that pleasure. Ultimately, God will win.

On December 5, 1931, Joseph Stalin had the largest Eastern Orthodox church in the world, the Cathedral of Christ our Savior, demolished. The cathedral had originally been built out of gratitude to God for allowing Russia to be rescued from Napoleon Bonaparte. Stalin had many churches demolished, but he had a special reason for this one. He wanted to replace the largest Orthodox church in the world with the tallest building in the world: the Palace of the Soviets, with a statue of Lenin on top.

But when they started to build, the soil under the cathedral proved unsuitable since it was too close to a river. After World War II, the Palace of the Soviets was never built. Instead, they built the largest outdoor pool in the world. But eventually even the pool was filled in with cement. And in 1995 at the exact same spot, and with a layout identical to the original, the Cathedral of Christ the Savior was rebuilt.[3] God will not be mocked! He will deliver.

Too often, when God does deliver His people, as He ultimately delivered David, we don't pause to publicly praise Him for His deliverance. He isn't given the credit. We just feel thankful and move on. But we are *called* to glorify God when He delivers. As David writes, "Let them shout for joy and rejoice, who favor my vindication; and let them say continually, 'The LORD be magnified, who delights in the prosperity of His servant.' And my tongue shall declare Your righteousness and Your praise all day long" (vv. 27–28).

Has God delivered you from something, rescued you, vindicated you in some way? What have you done about that? How have you thanked Him, praised Him, told others about His deliverance? Frankly, every Christian should be creating psalms of thanksgiving to God in one way or another. If we have asked God to deliver us and He has done so, we are under obligation not only to thank Him but to praise Him among the church—to advertise His goodness.

Where Is Jesus in Psalm 35?

Harry Ironside, in his commentary, said it best when he wrote, "Somebody has said, and I think rightly, that we may read this psalm as the musings of the heart of Jesus as He stood before Pilate's judgment seat. Read it at your leisure with that thought in mind. Say to yourself, 'I am going to think of this as though these words were uttered by the Lord Jesus as He stood before Pilate.' And I think you will see how aptly they would fit just such a case."[4]

I have done this, and it is remarkable how they fit the situation. And all these three prayers of David were remarkably similar to what our Lord must have been praying to His Father: "Heavenly Father, Fight the battles I can't. Deal with the unfairness I don't deserve, and vindicate me so I can publicly praise You." The Father answered them all, and He will do no less for you.

Jesus fought the battles we couldn't fight, lived the life we couldn't live, obeyed the Father when we couldn't. And He personally experienced unfairness we can't even imagine, receiving back, for His healing and loving ways, mocking, ridicule, beatings, and finally, execution. And in His death He vindicated us who didn't deserve vindication so that we could publicly praise Him for it.

Learn how to pray through the unfairness of life; God hears and answers those prayers. Let go of bitterness and anger; God will deal out punishment—no one is getting away with anything. In fact, if you knew what God was going to do to them, you would surely pity them. God is not mocked. And if you don't yet know Christ as your Savior, there are battles you can't win, unfairness you can't overcome, and vindication that will escape you—until you surrender to Him. Deliverance comes from the Lord, not from your own strength.

QUESTIONS

1. Everyone has experienced something that seems patently unfair. Can you remember a time when you experienced that, or are you are currently experiencing something? What is that thing, and why does it seem unfair? How do you think that sense of unfairness has affected your life?

2. Is there something right now that you are struggling with in which someone has done something evil to you (or continues to do so)? How have you responded to that so far? How have you prayed to God about this?

3. An anonymous author wrote, "If you don't heal from what hurt you, you'll bleed on those who didn't cut you." Is there a bitterness or hurt in your life that is still affecting you and as a result, affecting those who love you? Can you share this with others, and especially, with God?

4. David laments that those he treated with such mercy and grace have turned against him and treated him badly. They repaid him evil for good. Have you ever had someone you loved and trusted turn on you? How did it happen, and how did it affect you?

Chapter Seven

Gasping in Prayer . . .
When You're Drowning in Guilt

Psalm 38

When I was a singles pastor in Orange County, our singles group was spending the day at the beach one afternoon. It was hot, so a number of us decided to go body surfing. I had body surfed all my life, so it wasn't new to me, but one young man was from the Midwest.

As there is no ocean there, he had very little experience with the power of waves and the strong currents and riptides that can pull you quickly out to sea. And since he hadn't been around pools much either, he wasn't a strong swimmer. But he was tall enough to keep his feet on the sand. Until suddenly there was no sand under him. The riptide had carried him out to sea, along with myself. We didn't realize it until it was too late, and we were well over one hundred yards out.

When I looked at him, I realized he was in trouble. He was struggling. Have you ever seen anyone drowning? I have. My friend was drowning not more than five or six feet away from me. And I couldn't help him because I was tired myself. I can still see him going under the waves, coming up gasping for air, pawing at the water like a dog and then going under again and coming up again gasping, a look of desperation on his face.

He didn't know how to tread water. He didn't know how to float on his back. He didn't know how to swim out of the riptide. And he was, quite literally, going down for the third time. Fortunately, the lifeguards (so aptly named) had seen the danger and were already in the water. They pulled us both in—but I'll never forget the desperate look on his face, the desperate gasp for breath as he struggled to stay afloat.

When we read Psalm 38, we see someone going down for the third time, anchored to a sin that had dragged him to the very bottom of life. David is desperate, gasping in prayer because he was drowning in guilt. It is an experience any believer who has chosen to sin has experienced, and as such, it is instructive. David was gasping in prayer over . . .

The Desperate Consequences of Sin

When we see a child with a fork in their hand heading toward an open electrical socket, we instantly perceive the great danger they are in. The child doesn't. They have no idea of the consequences of what they are planning to do. So often when we dabble in sin, we are just like the children, ignorant of the terrible consequences of that action. But David knew what his current experiences were related to, so he wrote,

A Psalm of David, for a memorial.

O LORD, rebuke me not in Your wrath, and chasten me not in Your burning anger. For Your arrows have sunk deep into me, and Your hand has pressed down on me. There is no soundness in my flesh because of Your indignation; there is no health in my bones because of my sin. For my iniquities are gone over my head; as a heavy burden they weigh too much for me. My wounds grow foul and fester because of my folly. I am bent over and greatly bowed down; I go mourning all day long. For my loins are filled with burning, and there is no soundness in my flesh. I am benumbed and badly crushed; I groan because of the agitation of my heart. (vv. 1–8)

This psalm begins, "A Psalm of David, for a memorial." A memorial is something designed to make us remember something important. With God, a memorial means that He will not only *remember* your problem, but act on it. David is laying before God a serious problem he needs help with. He is asking God to remember his desperate need and rescue him. Every one of us can identify with that, so this psalm is also for us.

This is the cry of a man who is crushed by his sin and the consequences of it, who is confessing it to God and seeking forgiveness—and restoration! This is special and poignant. It is not common, sadly. You can see people today acting immorally who have no regrets or feelings of guilt about what they are doing. In place of sorrow is arrogance, and their moral conscience is calloused over years of ignoring it.

In today's culture, ironically, it is considered a strength that you no longer care about God or what anyone else feels about your moral choices. Moral failure has ceased to be a meaningful phrase to them. Yet here, one of the greatest warriors, one of the bravest men our world has ever known, David, is literally broken over some sin he has committed.

This is what we call conviction of sin. This is what is being described here. It's what the Holy Spirit of God produces in the heart of His children who wander, or run intentionally, into sin. Conviction is a brutally painful medicine—but so necessary. Without this experience we would continue to sin, unaware that it will lead to only worse consequences.

The Infection of Sin

If an arm or leg gets a bad infection and gangrene sets in, the doctor may need to cut off that limb to save the patient's life. To the onlooker it may seem an extreme solution, but it will be the difference between life and a painful, quick death. Some infections are so deep and serious, only desperate measures will save the patient.

Some people, unable to deal with the guilt and consequences of their sin, some evil they have done, end up taking their own lives. The behavior they thought they could get away with without any consequences has cast such a dark shadow on their lives and their futures, they see no hope—except in death as the final escape.

The Bible reminds us of the horrendous price of sin. It destroys our relationships with God and with others, and stains our consciences. In this psalm, when we see how deeply God pierces David's heart and conscience with guilt and grief, we can wonder if God isn't too harsh or David too sensitive. Neither is true. Sin is far more dangerous to us than we can possibly realize, and God far too kindly of a physician to allow the infection to spread without taking steps to stop it.

David does not seek to rationalize his sin or explain it away. He knows why he is miserable—"because of my sin . . . my iniquities . . . my folly . . ." The reason David is sad is because of his sin, period. It has affected his heart, his relationship with God, his relationships with others, and his physical health. The church needs to be reminded today that there is a terrible consequence for sin in the life of a believer. David wasn't an unbeliever—he was a believer! And *this* is how miserable sin will make a believer who consciously chooses sin over obedience. Listen to David: "Your arrows have sunk deep into me, . . . Your hand has pressed down on me. There is no soundness in my flesh because of your indignation; there is no health in my bones because of my sin. . . . My wounds grow foul and fester because of my folly" (vv. 2–5).

Like us, David had thought that indulging in his sin would be safe, that the most God might bring is a slight twinge of conscience, which he could deal with. Look again at these words.

The consequences of sin are not just cause and effect. This is so critical to understand. Cause and effect looks at the actions we initiate (cause) and what reaction (effect) that might provoke from others. We do something hurtful or thoughtless, and someone responds with anger and disappointment. Cause and effect. We think.

But it isn't. This is our Father's world! He is intimately involved with it. Every sin is against Him first, others second. He becomes actively involved in disciplining those who are His children—and not just through cause and effect. He brings guilt, shame, and discipline into our lives when we choose sin and ignore His warnings. He will effect circumstances in our lives—causing us to receive not blessings but discipline. Trouble. Problems. Sickness. Depression.

The consequences of sin are not just cause and effect but a surgical application of precisely what it will take for us to be able to see our sin and the pain it has produced. His goal is restoration, not judgment. Christ has already taken our judgment—but as Christians, we are His kids, and He will not allow us to sin with impunity. In Hebrews we are reminded,

> "My son, do not regard lightly the discipline of the LORD, nor faint when you are reproved by Him; for those whom the LORD loves He disciplines, and He scourges every son whom He receives." . . .
>
> All discipline for the moment seems not to be joyful, but sorrowful; yet to those who have been trained by it, afterwards it yields the peaceful fruit of righteousness. (12:5–6, 11)

Sin causes divine consequences that affect our mind, emotions, and body because we sin with our mind, emotions, and body. We see that in David's lament.

God's Sin-Alert System

David is feeling guilty . . . because he is guilty. He knows he has sinned. He isn't asking God why he is suffering—he knows why. "For my iniquities are gone over my head; as a heavy burden they weigh too much for me. My wounds grow foul and fester because of my folly. I am bent over and greatly bowed down; I go mourning all day long" (vv. 4–6).

God didn't create guilt just to make us feel bad—guilt is an emotion designed to alert us that we are in moral danger. Pain in our bodies is a signal that something is wrong. Pain is an alert; it prompts us to seek help. My pain led me to learn I had a bad gallbladder that needed to be removed. My pain led me to learn that I had a kidney stone, and through that, to learn that half of my kidneys were no longer functioning right. Pain is an alert that something somewhere is wrong.

Pain never says . . . nothing is wrong! Guilt is also an alert; it is the emotional equivalent of physical pain. Pain is a safety alert for our body. Guilt is a safety alert for our spirit. Both tell us we need healing. But there is a cure for guilt—the very thing David was seeking. We read in Hebrews 10:22 to "draw near with a sincere heart in full assurance of faith, having our hearts sprinkled clean from an evil conscience and our bodies washed with pure water." What can remove the emotional and spiritual pain of guilt is the faith that God can and will forgive us and make us clean again. So the apostle John wrote, "If we confess our sins, He is faithful and righteous to forgive us our sins and to cleanse us from all unrighteousness" (1 John 1:9).

> Pain is a safety alert for our body.
> Guilt is a safety alert for our spirit.

What grueling punishments does God demand from us when we sin against Him? Confession! When we agree with God that we have sinned, His promise—because Christ paid for our sins—is that He will not only forgive us but cleanse us. Cleanse us of what? The guilt!

There is a saying that a person "has blood on his hands." It means that he or she has done something that caused someone's death, either directly or indirectly. Now, there is no literal blood on their hands, but there is still an invisible stain of guilt.

We all have blood on our hands because it was our sin that led to Christ's sacrifice and death on the cross. Nothing we could do could remove that stain of guilt, so Jesus came and did what we couldn't. He used His precious and perfect blood to wipe clean the guilt that was ours. In the temple, the blood of a lamb was sprinkled on the mercy seat to bring forgiveness and cleansing. That's what Jesus did for us on the cross.

And when we receive Him as our Lord and Savior, He sprinkles His blood on our hearts, and His blood washes away our guilt. It was spiritual surgery—guilt was the required emotional pain telling us it was necessary.

"For my loins are filled with burning, and there is no soundness in my flesh. I am benumbed and badly crushed; I groan because of the agitation of my heart" (vv. 7–8). His sin has caused such turmoil within him that his body has gotten physically sick. Every part of him hurts and is in distress. David is gasping in prayer over the desperate consequences of his sin, but next we see David gasping in prayer over . . .

The Desperate Loneliness of Sin

There is not a place, a party, a game, a concert, a sensual experience . . . there is *nothing* that can diminish the loneliness that sin produces in the human heart. No one can understand what you are feeling and experiencing, and that makes the consequences of sin lonelier. So David writes,

> Lord, all my desire is before You, and my sighing is not hidden from You. My heart throbs, my strength fails me; and the light of my eyes, even that has gone from me. My loved ones and my friends stand aloof from my plague; and my kinsmen stand afar off. Those who seek my life lay snares for me; and those who seek to injure me have threatened destruction, and they devise treachery all day long. But I, like a deaf man, do not hear; and I am like a mute man who does not open his mouth. Yes, I am like a man who does not hear, and in whose mouth are no arguments. (vv. 9–14)

David is honest with God. He is saying, "You know what's going on inside me. All my desire is before You." God knows David's heart—that he wants to be restored to health and obedience and, most of all, joy.

"My sighing is not hidden from You. My heart throbs, my strength fails me; and the light of my eyes, even that has gone from me" (vv. 9–10). He recognizes that God alone knows how he really feels. And ultimately it is God he has sinned against, even though others were affected.

Only someone who has truly suffered deeply can understand this passage. There is a sigh that says *nothing* but communicates *everything*. It says hope is almost gone, our trouble is overwhelming, and we simply can't take any more. We're going down for the third time. We're all prayed out. A sigh is all we have left. Such are the heavy wages of sin in the life of a believer.

The proper pose before God when you have sinned is humility. David is experiencing real physical effects of the stress that sin has caused in his heart. The stress of sin is making him sicker and sicker, yet he realizes only the One he has sinned against can restore him! Counselors, therapists, and doctors can help us in many ways when we go through emotional issues. But when those struggles are the result of sin against God, the only cure, the only relief, comes from the One you have sinned against. He alone can fully restore you.

Bridging the Distance to God

If you have deeply offended a friend, coworker, or family member and are experiencing stress from that, a counselor or therapist can help you in some ways. But only by going to the one you have offended, and humbling yourself before them and asking forgiveness, can you hope to be restored to your previous relationship. The one you have offended holds the key to your recovery. Your counselor cannot make peace with your offended friend for you.

The stress is coming from the displeasure of the one you have offended—and will only be relieved when you humble yourself and seek forgiveness and reconciliation. And change your ways. This is a regular and frequent behavior in every good marriage. One or the other gets offended, hurt, and withholds their pleasure and acceptance. The other must recognize what they have done and seek reconciliation. Every. Single. Time.

It's the same with us and God. If you've ever felt someone's disapproval of you because you hurt them in some way, you know it creates a sense of distance between you. That easy and pleasant proximity you once shared with them is gone. You feel awkward and uncomfortable—and don't really want to be around them.

That's how people feel when they offend God by sin—they lose the sense of easy and pleasant intimateness they once enjoyed. Now what seems most comfortable is distance. But while it's more comfortable, it makes the relationship worse and makes it even harder to be reconciled. David continues, "My loved ones and my friends stand aloof from my plague; and my kinsmen stand afar off" (v. 11). You know things are going badly when even your friends desert you and your enemies want to kill you. And in Christ we have Someone who also experienced that horrible reality, don't we?

Because of David's sin, some were angry to the point of trying to kill him. "Those who seek my life lay snares for me; and those who seek to injure me have threatened destruction, and they devise treachery all day long" (v. 12). It makes us curious at what point in David's life this was, but we aren't told.

David does not threaten them back or ask God to judge and punish them. "But I, like a deaf man, do not hear; and I am like a mute man who does not open his mouth. Yes, I am like a man who does not hear, and in whose mouth are no arguments" (vv. 13–14).

David realized that he actually deserved what he was getting. Even if it seemed over the top, he understood that if he hadn't acted so badly, his enemies wouldn't feel the way they do about him. This started with his bad behavior—not theirs. Self-honesty is essential to healing from sin.

If you want to infuriate someone, just hurt them in some way, and then when they respond with anger and indignation, tell them to just cool their jets. Tell them they are overreacting. Encourage them to calm down. Because what that will say to them is that you are truly both clueless and callous to the pain you have caused them.

Now keep in mind that the sad and tragic distance David is describing here was all the result of a sin—first against God—and these powerful consequences are not just cause and effect. God uses relationships to discipline us when we sin against Him, because while all sin is against God, our sin also affects those around us. Sin leaves us gasping from the loneliness it produces in our lives. But lastly, we will see . . .

The Desperate Hope for Restoration

David is not hope*less* about his situation, but hope*ful* because he knows and understands the nature of his God. And he has experienced God's mercy and grace before, so he writes,

> For I hope in You, O Lord; You will answer, O Lord my God. For I said, "May they not rejoice over me, who, when my foot slips, would magnify themselves against me." For I am ready to fall, and my sorrow is continually before me. For I confess my iniquity; I am full of anxiety because of my sin. But my enemies are vigorous and strong, and many are those who hate me wrongfully. And those who repay evil for good, they oppose me, because I follow what is good. Do not forsake me, O Lord; O my God, do not be far from me! Make haste to help me, O Lord, my salvation! (vv. 15–22)

David understands how God responds to any who humble themselves before Him and turn away from their sin. As Proverbs 28:13 reminds us, "He who conceals his transgressions will not prosper, but he who confesses and forsakes them will find compassion."

And we are reminded that Jesus is the One who suffered for us, suffered what we should have—so no one understands the suffering of sin like Jesus. When you think He doesn't understand what you are going through, you are wrong. He went through the same thing on the cross with His Father. And whatever we suffer, we suffer for our *own* sin. Jesus suffered for *yours*.

Old Testament scholar Tremper Longman III wrote, "The difference between the godly and the wicked isn't that the latter sin while the former do not; but rather that the godly feel remorse that leads them to repentance and a desire to move closer to God." [1]

There were enemies David hadn't sinned against but who took great delight in seeing him fall. "For I said, 'May they not rejoice over me, who, when my foot slips, would magnify themselves against me.' For I am ready to fall" (vv. 16–17).

The prayer of David is that, despite his sin, God would not forsake him. David was not able to see as clearly as we can how great was God's grace and mercy. Jesus made it clear. The writer of Hebrews reminds us that "He Himself has said, 'I will never desert you, nor will I ever forsake you'" (13:5). The writer of Hebrews is quoting Jesus, but who was Jesus quoting when He said that? Jesus was, as usual, quoting the Old Testament.

We read in Deuteronomy 31:6, "Be strong and courageous, do not be afraid or tremble at them, for the LORD your God is the one who goes with you. He will not fail you or forsake you." And again in Joshua 1:5, "Just as I have been with Moses, I will be with you; I will not fail you or forsake you." God is the same yesterday, today, and forever!

David's last-gasp hope was in God—that God would restore him and one day soon the pain would be gone and the joy would return. David was literally gasping for that day.

David was gasping in prayer, but he knew God would answer him and give him grace and mercy.

Where Is Jesus in Psalm 38?

This whole psalm becomes powerful when you imagine Jesus in the garden of Gethsemane, before His enemies at His trial, in front of Pilate and Herod, and on the cross. Can you see Jesus in the garden in verses 7–8? "For my loins are filled with burning, and there is no soundness in my flesh. I am benumbed and badly crushed; I groan because of the agitation of my heart."

Can you see Jesus on trial in verses 11, 13–14? "My loved ones and my friends stand aloof from my plague, and my kinsmen stand afar off. . . . But I, like a deaf man, do not hear; and I am like a mute man who does not open his mouth. Yes, I am like a man who does not hear, and in whose mouth are no arguments."

Can you see Jesus on the cross in verses 17, 19–21? "For I am ready to fall, and my sorrow is continually before me. . . . But my enemies are vigorous and strong, and many are those who hate me wrongfully. And those who repay evil for good, they oppose me because I follow what is good. Do not forsake me, O LORD; O my God, do not be far from me!"

Maybe as you read this, you are a Christian gasping in prayer. There is a sin, known only to you, that you have not abandoned. It is eating away at you. You have lost the joy of your salvation. God is calling you to restoration. But you need to abandon that sin and ask for His help in forsaking it completely. God is rich (not stingy) in mercy!

But you need to confess your sin to Him, and others if necessary. Let it go.

It's killing you right now. And if you don't have the strength, and we often don't, ask God to show His power in your weakness to help you. Claim what the apostle Paul did in 2 Corinthians 12:9: "And He has said to me, 'My grace is sufficient for you, for power is perfected in weakness.'"

If you don't yet know Christ as your Savior, you are drowning in sins you can't atone for, but Jesus already did! He wants you to ask Him for mercy, grace, and peace. He will give it to you. Come to Him. Call to Him. Even if all you can manage is a sigh or a gasp, He will hear it and answer you with grace.

QUESTIONS

1. We are often told that feelings of guilt are unhealthy, yet God left us a powerful example of a man sharing his guilt over a sin. What do you think the Bible teaches are the differences between a healthy guilt, and an unhealthy guilt over sin?

2. Sin makes us miserable, besides the conviction of sin that God can bring. How has your own sin in the past made you miserable? How did it affect the enjoyment and pleasure of your life?

3. Self-honesty is essential to healing from sin and its consequences. Why do you think it's so hard to be honest about our sins to others and to God? What are we afraid of?

Chapter Eight

Gaining Traction When Life Goes off the Rails

Psalm 40

Our family once drove to South Lake Tahoe for a vacation. It was winter, but most of the snow had melted. We decided to take a drive up to Fallen Leaf Lake, a pristine alpine lake perched above Lake Tahoe.

At the time we had a minivan, and though the road was narrow and rough, we were actually enjoying the ups and downs of the primitive road until we came to a rather wide depression.

We started down it carefully, and when we got to the bottom, I accelerated to get us back up the other side. No go! The wheels spun as the back end slid. I climbed out in the frigid air and realized we had landed on a thick piece of ice.

I could turn the steering wheel any way I wanted, I could hit the accelerator, but all I got was spinning wheels. None of the ways formerly available to me to control my car worked anymore. I even tried putting sticks and twigs under the tires to help them gain traction. Nothing helped.

No matter what we tried, I couldn't gain any traction. Then I had to do what I loathed doing—put on the tire chains. Have you ever tried putting on tire chains when your hands are freezing and your tires are sitting on a piece of ice—and you aren't really good at putting on chains? It was a great challenge to my sanctification. Fortunately, we got them on enough to get us out of that depression.

There have been other times when my life entered a bit of a depression—when no matter what I tried, my life wouldn't gain any traction. None of the ways I had formerly controlled my life were available to me anymore. I saw no way out of the pit and no way back where I had come from. I couldn't go forward, and I couldn't go back. I tried everything I could think of . . . and nothing. Maybe you've been there. Maybe you are there now.

Psalm 40 is David's testimony of how he gained traction when his life went off the rails. And David is going to show us that gaining traction involves telling God three things, beginning with . . .

You Delivered Me Marvelously

David's faith that God would meet his need was premised on the experiences he had with God in the past. If you depended on someone, and they failed you, you don't usually return to them for help. But that hadn't been David's experience. So David writes,

I waited patiently for the LORD; and He inclined to me and heard my cry. He brought me up out of the pit of destruction, out of the miry clay, and He set my feet upon a rock making my footsteps firm. He put a new song in my mouth, a song of praise to our God; many will see and fear and will trust in the LORD. How blessed is the man who has made the LORD his trust, and has not turned to the proud, nor to those who lapse into falsehood. Many, O LORD my God, are the wonders which You have done, and Your thoughts toward us; there is none to compare with You. If I would declare and speak of them, they would be too numerous to count. Sacrifice and meal offering You have not desired; my ears You have opened; burnt offering and sin offering You have not required. Then I said, "Behold, I come; in the scroll of the book it is written of me. I delight to do Your will, O my God; Your Law is within my heart." (vv. 1–8)

The phrase "I waited patiently" is literally translated in the Hebrew, "I *waited—waited*." When a word is repeated like that, it conveys intensity and significance. In other words, the waiting isn't passive ("I waited, because what else could I do?") but active and intense ("I waited, because I was *eagerly anticipating* something").

When David could not find any footing and everything was uncertain in his life, he intently waited upon God, because he trusted God would soon bring the direction and stability he needed. And he had experienced God doing just that. "And He inclined to me and heard my cry. He brought me up out of the pit of destruction, out of the miry clay, and He set my feet upon a rock making my footsteps firm" (v. 2).

There are times when all the things we are attempting to get out of our problems are failing, nothing in our life is settled, everything is up in the air. Everywhere we step is unstable. That's what David is describing here. "Miry clay" was wet spongy earth, deep mud, or slush. It's the picture of a person trying to slosh through mud to find something solid to stand on and being continually frustrated.

But God met David there. God took pity on David and settled his life. He helped David gain traction and find answers, solutions, insights, direction, and provision. David finally felt secure and stable again. It's a wonderful feeling when life begins to be predictable again, safe, secure. The result was that "He put a new song in my mouth, a song of praise to our God" (v. 3).

I clearly remember a time when so much of my life was up in the air—my job, where we were supposed to live, our future, our living arrangement, our finances. And the worst thing was that I couldn't do anything about any of it. It was one of the most trying times of my life.

I like ruts, familiarity, predictability, to feel as if I have some control over my life. All of that was taken from me. My feet were stuck in sloshy and gooey circumstances, and I could not gain any traction. All I could do was pray God would help me. I had to wait far longer than I thought was necessary, and I despaired at times. And my personality doesn't lend itself to despair—I'm an eternal optimist. But this was a dark time.

And then God delivered me. And He not only delivered me, He gave me far more than I had been hoping for. Only then could I see what God had been doing the whole time was preparing to bless me. And as David says, God "put a new song in my mouth, a song of praise to our God."

I needed to learn I could trust God for everything and anything. And while God blessed me materially, the greatest blessing was not material—it was the strong foundation I discovered for my faith in God. That's where I most needed stability; I see that now. When was the last time you thanked God for delivering you? We need to see that God is our solid rock. Edward Mote wrote, in his great hymn "The Solid Rock,"

My hope is built on nothing less
Than Jesus' blood and righteousness;
I dare not trust the sweetest frame,
But wholly lean on Jesus' name.

On Christ, the solid Rock, I stand;
All other ground is sinking sand,
All other ground is sinking sand.

When darkness veils His lovely face,
I rest on His unchanging grace;
In every high and stormy gale,
My anchor holds within the veil.

His oath, His covenant, His blood
Support me in the whelming flood;
When all around my soul gives way,
He then is all my hope and stay.

When He shall come with trumpet sound,
Oh, may I then in Him be found;
Dressed in His righteousness alone,
Faultless to stand before the throne.

"On Christ the solid rock I stand, all other ground is sinking sand. All other ground is sinking sand."

These words echo the words of David.

The New Song

Harry Ironside wrote of the "new song" in the first stanza of Psalm 40:

> The new song is the song of redemption. Naturally when we read of a new song, the question arises in our minds, what is the old song? The old song is the song of creation. Away back in the book of Job we read, "Where wast thou when I laid the foundations of the earth? . . . when the morning stars sang together, and all the sons of God shouted for joy?" (Job 38:4, 7). What a song that was when this world in all its pristine beauty sprang fresh from its Maker's hands and went circling off into space! Holy angels in rapture sang at the sight of it and all the hosts of God shouted for joy; but that song soon died away into a sad, bitter wail, for sin came in and blighted that fair creation, and God was dishonored in the universe He had made. Then our Lord Jesus came and He went down into the depths into which sin had cast men in order that He might lift us out. He went to the cross to glorify God who had been so terribly dishonored by man's sin and folly. And when He came forth from the tomb He was prepared to start the new creation singing.[1]

When we get to Revelation 5:9–10 we read, "And they sang a new song, saying, 'You are worthy to take the scroll and to open its seals; for You were slain and have redeemed us to God with Your blood out of every tribe and tongue and people and nation'" (NKJV).

And how did God meet David's needs? He responded to David's trust; He blessed David's integrity. In the unstable period of his life, when it would have been so easy to take a shortcut or turn away from God, he continued to trust in God. "Many will see and fear and will trust in the LORD. How blessed is the man who has made the LORD his trust, and has not turned to the proud, nor to those who lapse into falsehood" (vv. 3–4).

There are those who claim to be able to meet our needs themselves. If we would just listen to their inspired wisdom, we would never go wrong, they tell us. They are proud and arrogant—feeling they have all the answers. Those voices can be found in politics, philosophy, sports, music, economics, and pulpits. They urge you to follow them—but David sees through that. He continues, "Many, O LORD my God, are the wonders which You have done, and Your thoughts toward us; there is none to compare with You. If I would declare and speak of them, they would be too numerous to count" (v. 5).

David didn't just thank God for His deliverance—he thought deeply about it. He marveled at how God needed to choreograph so many things to help him.

How many computer commands are necessary to make a robot take a single step? Thousands, maybe tens of thousands? And life is far more complex than that. You can limit the robot's exposure to other factors, but you can't do that in real life.

The moment we step out the door in the morning, there are thousands upon thousands of factors that can affect our day and life: people, things, weather, traffic, wildlife, viruses, germs, and so many others. Any and all of these things can affect us positively or negatively—or both. David thought about God. He paid attention to what God did in his life. Do we?

When I think of all the steps necessary to make sure I met my wife, Annette, and married her, I stand amazed. Things had to happen before either of us was even born to ensure that we would not only meet one day in El Toro, California, but both be believers in Jesus Christ, and on top of that ensure that when we met, we would truly be what the other wanted and needed.

Had I met Annette three years earlier, would we have even been attracted to each other? We would likely have had little in common and would have been running in different circles, with different ideas about life and its true purpose.

Had my parents not moved us to Palos Verdes Peninsula when I was in junior high, would I have ever gone to the little Baptist church and met the people who would so profoundly affect my life? Would I have ever even thought about God, who was not even on my radar?

Had I not married Annette, and as a result visited her grandparents in Solvang, California, and consequently fallen in love with the Santa Ynez Valley, would we have ever moved there when we left Southern California? And if we hadn't, would I have ever come in contact with Shoreline Community Church, the church that has meant so much to me these last twenty years? And yet I did. I was supposed to go there—but wow, all the complexity and choreography necessary to make all that happen is mind-boggling. "Many, O LORD my God, are the wonders which You have done, and Your thoughts toward us; there is none to compare with You. If I would declare and speak of them, they would be too numerous to count" (v. 5).

Have you thought of revisiting the wonderful acts of God in your past just to thank God and praise Him? Have you considered how God loves to hear our praise? David continues, "Sacrifice and meal offering You have not desired; my ears You have opened; burnt offering and sin offering You have not required" (v. 6).

What does this mean? Sacrifices and offerings were like IOUs to God. They did not remove sin or guilt—they just covered them over until they would one day finally be dealt with. In a sense, every Israelite came and gave their sacrifices and offerings to God, admitting they were in debt to Him. And when they did, the Lord, in a sense, endorsed them all, saying, "One day I will settle this bill."

On the cross, the debts finally met the payment. Jesus came and took all our IOUs and took them to the cross. He was the final and complete payment all the sacrifices had looked forward to. It's why, when He hung on the cross, He uttered the words, "It is finished." In the Greek, *tetelestai*, meaning "paid in full."

How could one sacrifice atone for all those sins? It's because our sins, as great as they were, were finite. In an average life of seventy or eighty years we will sin a very specific amount of times, but death will finally end that. The number is computable. But Jesus's obedience was, because of His divine nature, infinite. God received far greater glory from Jesus's obedience than His nature was offended by our sins. Just offering sacrifices and offerings, however, without a heart that correspondingly wanted to please God, was unacceptable. David continues, "Then I said, 'Behold, I come; in the scroll of the book it is written of me. I delight to do Your will, O my God; Your Law is within my heart'" (vv. 7–8).

The scroll was the law of God, and David was saying that he not only approved and obeyed the law, but that he loved it. He had put it in his heart. Sacrifices were to be an outer expression of an inner faith. As the prophet Samuel said, "Has the LORD as much delight in burnt offerings and sacrifices as in obeying the voice of the LORD? Behold, to obey is better than sacrifice, and to heed than the fat of rams" (1 Samuel 15:22).

Where Is Jesus in Psalm 40?

The New Testament quotes this passage to speak of a greater David, a greater King who was foreshadowed in Psalm 40 by David. The writer of Hebrews explained:

> Therefore, when He comes into the world, He says, "Sacrifice and offering You have not desired, but a body You have prepared for Me; in whole burnt offerings and sacrifices for sin You have taken no pleasure. Then I said, 'Behold, I have come (in the scroll of the book it is written of Me) to do Your will, O God.'" After saying above, "Sacrifices and offerings and whole burnt offerings and sacrifices for sin You have not desired, nor have You taken pleasure in them" (which are offered according to the Law), then He said, "Behold, I have come to do Your will." He takes away the first in order to establish the second. By this will we have been sanctified through the offering of the body of Jesus Christ once for all. (10:5–10)

In John 8:29 Jesus said, "For I always do the things that are pleasing to Him." But doing the will of God involves doing not only what God approves but what He appoints. Think of our Lord. He loved the law of God—what God approved. But He also had to go to the cross, and He didn't want to do it. He struggled greatly in Gethsemane. He did not only what God approved but what God appointed Him to do.

> Doing the will of God involves doing not only what God approves but what He appoints.

Obedience to God involves us doing not only what God approves—His law—but also what He appoints us to do in life. I experienced three broken homes in my past, and it was horrible. I would never want to experience that again, but I would also never undo it. I needed it all. It matured me, strengthened me, and made me more like Jesus than I was. It was not pleasant, but it was oh so necessary. David gains traction in life by remembering how God marvelously delivered him once, but then he tells God, in essence, "I praised You then as I praise You now" (see v. 9).

A huge part of David's ability to gain traction was that he never forgot what God had done in his life and never stopped praising Him for it. So we read,

> I have proclaimed glad tidings of righteousness in the great con-gregation; behold, I will not restrain my lips, O LORD, You know. I have not hidden Your righteousness within my heart; I have spoken of Your faithfulness and Your salvation; I have not concealed Your lovingkindness and Your truth from the great congregation.
>
> You, O LORD, will not withhold Your compassion from me; Your lovingkindness and Your truth will continually preserve me. (vv. 9–11)

Look at David's words: "I have proclaimed . . . I will not restrain my lips . . . I have not hidden. . . . I have spoken . . . I have not concealed." David was not quiet when God blessed him, rescued him, and helped him. He was a spokes-man for God's goodness. Are we? Do we tell people what God has done in our lives? Do we tell others what He is doing?

One of the most frequent questions a person is asked is, "How are you doing?" It's a common greeting. How often when we hear that question do we take the opportunity to publicly praise and thank God for what He has done in our lives? What did David tell people about God? He told them about God's righteousness . . . His faithfulness . . . His salvation . . . His lovingkindness . . . His truth. And why did he do that? As David says, it's because "You, O LORD, will not withhold Your compassion from me; Your lovingkindness and Your truth will continually preserve me" (v. 11).

God sustains David with compassion, lovingkindness, and truth. When David got tired and discouraged, it wasn't his strong personality and willpower that sustained him, and he knew it.

When you get tired and discouraged and lose hope, where do you go look-ing for hope and strength? Motivational speakers? Popular gurus? Political lead-ers? Celebrities? Friends and family? Each of these may be able to give you their own insight and knowledge that may contain elements of truth, wisdom, and insight, yet only in God can you find ultimate truth, wisdom, and insight, com-bined with a perfect and eternal love for you.

It was John Newton, former slave trader and author of the song "Amazing Grace," who once was reported as saying, "I have reason to praise Him for my trials, for, most probably, I should have been ruined without them."

David praised God when God rescued him, and he praised God when rescue was not yet apparent. His praise to God was in a sure hope. But the final way that David gains traction when his life goes off the rails is by telling God, "I need to be marvelously delivered . . . again!"

When David faced instability and his life went off the rails, he learned to look into the past, live in the present praising God, and have confidence in the future God had for him. So he writes,

> For evils beyond number have surrounded me; my iniquities have overtaken me, so that I am not able to see; they are more numerous than the hairs of my head, and my heart has failed me. Be pleased, O LORD, to deliver me; make haste, O LORD, to help me. Let those be ashamed and humiliated together who seek my life to destroy it; let those be turned back and dishonored who delight in my hurt. Let those be appalled because of their shame who say to me, "Aha, aha!" Let all who seek You rejoice and be glad in You; let those who love Your salvation say continually, "The LORD be magnified!" Since I am afflicted and needy, let the Lord be mindful of me. You are my help and my deliverer; do not delay, O my God. (vv. 12–17)

David has shown in the first part of this psalm the rewards and blessings that come from waiting on God. Now he reminds us that those kinds of situations will come again. We will one day find ourselves once again needing to wait upon God for deliverance. Yet this time we will be different than the first time.

We will have a deeper sense of God's unmerited grace. We will have grown to love our salvation, to rejoice and be glad in God, even while we have to wait for Him to open doors, close doors, and put us on solid ground again. We can even now, in the midst of our problems, say, "The Lord be magnified!"

And we have also learned by experience that God listens to and responds to the "afflicted and needy." The Lord thinks about our needs. He is "mindful of me." He is our "helper and deliverer." Unless you come to know God this way, you will never find peace when life is unpeaceful. You'll believe inner peace can only come when everything is all worked out. We need to know that although we are "afflicted and needy," God is our "help and deliverer."

But in verses 11–12, David reminds us that many of our troubles and problems are of our own making. We contributed greatly to the issues we are now facing with decisions we made, things we said, things we did, things we didn't say, and things we didn't do. "My iniquities have overtaken me, so that I am not able to see; they are more numerous than the hairs of my head, and my heart has failed me" (v. 12).

He wasn't afraid to honestly confess his failures to God. Are we? He urges us to in the Psalms. It blesses Him and heals us.

At times, though, we find it difficult to be honest with God and ourselves. In life we battle against two enemies perpetually: the enemy without (those who wish us harm) and the enemy within (ourselves). We are often our own worst enemy. Fortunately, God delivers us from both enemies: foreign and domestic. Isn't that great to know? Even when we are the fault of the stress we are under, still He comes to rescue us. Do you understand God that way?

I think of our firefighters, police officers, and health-care professionals. They have such difficult jobs. They are expected to rescue us from fires that would destroy us, criminals who would harm us, and sickness that would kill us (enemies from without). But they are also called upon to rescue us from fires and dangers caused by our own foolishness at times (the enemy within). Police officers are frequently called to calm down problems that began in our own homes. And health-care professionals frequently have to warn us that we are the greatest problem to our physical health and safety by our bad health habits. Yet they rescue us anyway. So does God.

And when we act foolishly, there are those who love to kick us when we're down. "Let those be ashamed and humiliated together who seek my life to destroy it; let those be turned back and dishonored who delight in my hurt. Let those be appalled because of their shame who say to me, 'Aha, aha!'" (vv. 14–15).

Problems are intensified when those who don't like us enjoy our suffering. And say so publicly.

We want life to be smooth, solid, stable, and predictable. But it isn't. And our desires for that perfect life are often the problem. As Pastor John Piper has written, "If I am to love like Jesus loved, my ravenous craving for a trouble-free life must die."[2] To chase a trouble-free life in this world is like trying to catch your shadow. That trouble-free world awaits us—it's not here yet.

Gaining traction when life goes off the rails involves telling God this: "You delivered me marvelously once. I praised you then, as I praise you now, but I need to be marvelously delivered again."

And maybe that's precisely where you are today and precisely what you need to do. Why not take a quiet moment right now and pray this kind of prayer to God? "Lord, You delivered me marvelously once, and I praised you then. It's harder to praise You now because my fears would muzzle my praise. But I am going to trust You and ask You to marvelously deliver me once again. And when You do, I promise to praise You again!"

"On Christ the solid rock I stand, all other ground is sinking sand. All other ground is sinking sand." And if you don't know Christ as your savior, you still have an outstanding IOU to God for the payment of your sins. You need Jesus to pay it for you. He has already done it, but you have to accept it by faith and surrender your will to Jesus. Will you do that today?

It can be done in the simplest prayer to God. As we have seen, He wants us to talk with Him. He is, in fact, waiting for it.

QUESTIONS

1. Are there things in life that are harder for you to trust God for than others? What are they, and why do you think they are harder for you?

2. Take some time and write down three times when you feel God really delivered you in a special way. Did you take the time to praise Him for those? If you didn't, take the time now. Revisit that moment. See its implications, and praise Him for what He has done. Be honest and grateful! God loves our gratitude.

3. When was the last time you told someone what God had done or was doing in your life? If you have, what was it? If you haven't, ask God to give you the courage to begin sharing His wonderful works in your life that He might be glorified.

Chapter Nine

The Anatomy of Despair:
Too Little God, Too Much Stress

Psalm 42

Kimberli Lira was a young mother with two young children and a husband, a believer who battled acute lymphoblastic lymphoma until he died of it. She was left with huge medical bills, the sole responsibility of raising her two children, and no husband to love and help her and be her companion.

She couldn't help but notice how many churches were trying so many gimmicks to attract people. She tried to help the churches understand that when the bottom has fallen out of life and you have no strength left, gimmicks aren't what you need. She wrote in her blog about lying in bed and listening to her daughter sob uncontrollably because she missed her father so much. In light of that, learning that her church leaders were reading the latest "how to grow your church" books wasn't comforting.

Cool sermon series topics and the minister relating the message to a Hollywood film didn't help her. All she could think of was how desperately she needed Jesus:

There are days I am running on empty and a coffee bar in the lobby isn't filling me up. There are days when the pain is so brutal and a concert like setting is not providing healing. There are days when the tears won't stop and a trendsetting church is not what I need. I need Jesus. . . .

There are people whose marriages are crumbling, people whose finances are deteriorating, . . . and people like me, whose husband has passed away after a brutal fight with cancer. And these people are not impressed with the stage lighting. . . . They don't need to be pumped or hyped. They need and are desperate for Jesus.[1]

And we come to Psalm 42, where the psalmist is not expressing anger but *longing*. He is despairing because he has too little God and too much stress. What can you say when that is true? How do you respond? Many of us are there or have been there. In Psalm 42 we see the anatomy of despair. The anatomy of despair starts with . . .

Thirsting for the Presence of God: "Too Little God"

When you've experienced the deep joy to be found in God's presence, in His pleasure in your life, in His blessings upon you, and then you go through turmoil that removes that from you, what you want more than anything is to get back there. But how? That was David's question:

For the choir director. A Maskil of the sons of Korah.

As the deer pants for the water brooks, so my soul pants for You, O God. My soul thirsts for God, for the living God; when shall I come and appear before God? My tears have been my food day and night, while they say to me all day long, "Where is your God?" These things I remember and I pour out my soul within me. For I used to go along with the throng and lead them in procession to the house of God, with the voice of joy and thanksgiving, a multitude keeping festival.

Why are you in despair, O my soul? And why have you become disturbed within me? Hope in God, for I shall again praise Him for the help of His presence. O my God, my soul is in despair within me;

therefore I remember You from the land of the Jordan and the peaks
of Hermon, from Mount Mizar. (vv. 1–6)

The psalmist, despite his problems, has not given up on his belief in God—
but he is missing his wonderful experience with God. He remembers when it
gave him such joy and comfort and purpose. But that part of his relationship
with God seems gone. Circumstances have seemingly changed all that.

The psalmist at some point in his life had seen a deer panting for water
in the Middle Eastern heat. That poignant image stayed with him, and now
he remembers that scene and says, "That's how thirsty I feel for the presence of God in my life. That's the perfect picture of my soul's longing." The
deer remembers the stream, the water hole, and longs for it. "My soul thirsts for
God, for the living God" (v. 2). The psalmist isn't afraid to speak to God this
way, this intimately. He longs for God more than any human presence.

"When shall I come and appear before God?" (v. 2). The psalmist could
pray to God anytime, but the only way to appear before Him was at the tabernacle, or the temple. The history of this psalm suggests that the psalmist had
for some reason been unable to attend the tabernacle. He was probably in some
kind of danger from enemies within Israel itself. So the very place he most
wants to be, the place he most associates with the presence of God and joy in
his life, he can't go.

"My soul thirsts for God, for the living God" (v. 2). In the psalmist's day,
every nation had their gods of wood and stone they cried to for help. But the
psalmist knew there was only one God, the living God. He needed to touch
the living God. Life needs to touch life to have meaning. It's not enough to
accumulate things and accomplish things. For us to find true joy and peace, our
soul—and not merely our human drives—needs to be touched.

Only too recently, because of a pandemic, many of our people faced the
same dilemma. They missed church. They could pray to God, and they did.
And they could watch the services live stream, and they did. But they found
themselves, like the psalmist, unable to come to church, to join the fellowship
praising God together—that in-person fellowship is so powerful and healing.
Virtual church can never provide that. "When shall I come and appear before
God?"

A Deep Mystery

"My tears have been my food day and night" (v. 3). When the psalmist says his tears have been his food day and night, those tears are related to the loss of his fellowship with his God. Deep in every human soul is the need for God. As the geese are impelled to fly south for the winter, as the salmon feel impelled to leave their streams and swim to the vast oceans, as the bee feels impelled to leave the hive, so the human soul feels impelled to return to its God.

It's a deep mystery—and every human soul feels it—but they don't know what they are feeling. Do the monarch butterflies that migrate thousands of miles understand what drives them to do it? They brave danger and death—but they are driven on by something they don't understand.

Because our culture has convinced itself there is no God, or if there is a God, He can be (and is) created and designed by the human mind, they too feel the deep longing, but can't properly respond to it.

They try to understand why they are so unhappy, discontent, empty—even when they are prosperous, successful, and entertain themselves constantly. But still there is the lingering emptiness. They try to anesthetize it—drink it away, smoke it away, sniff it away, vacation it away, accomplish it away, produce it away, accumulate it away, educate it away, protest it away, politicize it away . . . but nothing works.

Our soul was meant to return to God the way the geese were meant to migrate to their home, the salmon to their stream, the bees to their hive. God created us that way, and whether we choose to believe in Him or not, that is the reality we face.

There is a reason we always seem to want more than we have. There is a reason no amount of money or success or popularity can satisfy us. There is a reason we still yearn for something we can't quite put our finger on—something deeper and more important than stuff, success, and celebrity.

When I say this, I am not speaking of simply the nonbeliever but the believer as well. The believer now has Jesus, and He is our all—but we still see Him at a distance and want to be so much nearer to Him. We know now the only place perfect uninterrupted joy can be found, but even we yearn to join Him, to begin our new life in His very presence. When you truly love someone, you want to grow closer to them all the time.

When sin interrupts the believer's sweet fellowship with God, and trouble and enemies and sickness and pain and loss challenge our joy and peace, we yearn to return completely to God, to enter the eternal joy, the eternal peace, where those things can no longer touch us. Until we leave this body, we will always thirst for God. We will always want more of Him and less of this world.

The geese that migrate south soon feel the need to reverse course. The salmon that felt impelled to leave their home now feel impelled to return. The bees that leave the hive now go in search of it again. We are all following the mystery of God, trying to return to what we once had. God imprinted our souls to need Him and search for Him. We were made in His image and long to return to Him.

Until you understand this truth, you will always wonder why you have some of the feelings that you do. And you will never know the true cure for the sickness of the soul—that deep soul thirst.

"While they say to me all day long, 'Where is your God?'" (v. 3). If you are in the least public about your faith in Christ, and share your victories in Him, those who don't believe in God often can't wait to pounce on your troubles. "Hey, I thought your God could fix everything! How's that 'God thing' working out for you now, hmm?"

> These things I remember and I pour out my soul within me. For I used to go along with the throng and lead them in procession to the house of God, with the voice of joy and thanksgiving, a multitude keeping festival. (v. 4)

There was a time when the psalmist was in a position to lead the procession of people going up to Jerusalem, to the tabernacle or temple, possibly at Passover, Pentecost, or a Feast of Booths festival. In those times people streamed into Jerusalem with shouting, praising, and joy. That was a mountaintop experience, and now it is gone and he wants it back desperately.

Our Churning Place

The psalmist understands his present problems won't continue. Life is a series of tunnels we go through and then come out of. In my life I have gone through countless tunnels that stole my happiness. And each one felt like it would never end.

Every single one did.

It's why the psalmist speaks to his soul, answering his fears. "Why are you in despair, O my soul? And why have you become disturbed within me? Hope in God, for I shall again praise Him for the help of His presence" (v. 5). Here is found healthy biblical self-talk.

Charles Swindoll wrote,

I have a "churning place." It is in my stomach. On the upper, left side, just below the rib cage. When disturbing things happen, when troubling words are said, when certain letters that contain ugly words are written or extremely critical comments are read, my inner churning starts. Do you have something similar?

One friend of mine says his spot is in his head, specifically his forehead. Another told me his "churning place" resides at the back of his neck. Most people I know have a particular region where grinding occurs, usually triggered by . . . bad news, personal conflict, unpaid bills, legal problems, expensive repairs, difficult decisions, impossible deadlines, unresolved sin. I find it rather comforting that God's inspired hymnal does not omit the grind of inner turmoil.[2]

Despair in the Hebrew means "to crouch down, bow down, to be low and abased." It speaks of those days when we want to curl up in the fetal position and pretend life away. So David speaks to his fear and says, "Therefore I remember You" (v. 6). This is what fear never wants you to do—change the subject. Because when you change the subject and pray to God, you may change your perspective as well. Fear needs constant attention to have its full effect on us.

It's why he asks, "Why are you in despair, O my soul?" (v. 5). That question is relevant only if he is thinking of the good things God has done for him in the past. He is saying what we need to say, "Hey soul, stop shaking long enough to remember that we've been here before, and God has always rescued us."

The psalmist speaks to his soul . . . answering his fears. "Hope in God, for I shall again praise Him for the help of His presence . . ." He says, "Hey fears— God will do something that will make you praise Him again. Hey fears—no matter how scary you are—my hope is in God. Soul, remember this—God will rescue you. The tunnel *will* end!"

The psalmist is going through trouble, but his main concern is that he misses the presence of God in his life, that feeling that he used to have with

God, the feeling of safety and security and assurance. He wants it back. But now we see the other side of the anatomy of despair . . .

Drowning in the Problems of Life: "Too Much Stress!"

When you are overwhelmed with trouble and stress, you feel like you are drowning in sorrow and there is no one to help you. Despair becomes your dominant emotion. You just can't seem to generate any hope that it's going to get better. The psalmist knows this feeling, and writes,

> Deep calls to deep at the sound of Your waterfalls; all Your breakers and Your waves have rolled over me. The LORD will command His lovingkindness in the daytime; and His song will be with me in the night, a prayer to the God of my life.
> I will say to God my rock, "Why have You forgotten me? Why do I go mourning because of the oppression of the enemy?" As a shattering of my bones, my adversaries revile me, while they say to me all day long, "Where is your God?" Why are you in despair, O my soul? And why have you become disturbed within me? Hope in God, for I shall yet praise Him, the help of my countenance and my God. (vv. 7–11)

In the early verses, the psalmist had written, "Therefore I remember You from the land of the Jordan and the peaks of Hermon, from Mount Mizar" (v. 6). The psalmist remembers traveling from Jerusalem to northern Galilee, where the Jordan River originates on Mount Hermon. The psalmist imagines himself on one of the small peaks in the Mount Hermon range.

As the snow melts on those peaks, it travels downhill, creating streams and waterfalls, thundering down the mountain. All that water is a picture of the troubles he's experiencing. "Deep calls to deep at the sound of Your waterfalls; all Your breakers and Your waves have rolled over me" (v. 7).

The word *deep* refers most likely to a wave, a rolling body of water that might be seen crashing down a mountain from the peaks above. The idea is that the torrents of water just keep coming, and each wave represents a problem to him. One problem bumps into another problem in his life until he is overwhelmed. "Deep calls to deep," or as we might say, "Man, it's just one thing after another—it just never ends." We frequently talk about a "flood" of tears or a "flood" of grief. The idea is we have more problems than we can handle.

Earlier, water was a picture of what he needed; now it is a picture of what is overwhelming him. But the psalmist finds hope. "The LORD will command His lovingkindness in the daytime; and His song will be with me in the night, a prayer to the God of my life" (v. 8).

The psalmist hopes and prays that God will meet him at his point of greatest need, brighten his day, encourage his soul. It is a prayer for emotional support. We often need hope even before we need help. The answer, the rescue, will come—we believe this, but what we need at the moment is hope!

From his own experience, Charles Spurgeon wrote,

> Our longest sorrows have a close, and there is a bottom to the profoundest depths of our misery. Our winters shall not frown forever; summer will soon smile. The tide shall not eternally ebb out; the floods retrace their march. The night shall not hang its darkness forever over our souls; the sun shall yet arise with healing beneath his wings. [3]

In Sheldon Vanauken's book *A Severe Mercy*, he tells of the overwhelming grief he suffered after the death of his wife, Davy. He felt completely alone in the world, without the comfort of God or man. One night, as he lie awake thinking, he decided to completely reject God, to turn his back on his faith. And he tried. He really did. But no matter how much Sheldon tried to reject God, no matter how much he tried to deny His existence, he found he just couldn't do it. His faith was so ingrained in his heart and mind and spirit, so much a part of his every fiber, that it didn't do any good to deny it. He simply couldn't reject God, even when he tried. [4]

Yet, the psalmist shared honestly what life felt like at the moment. "I will say to God my rock, 'Why have You forgotten me? Why do I go mourning because of the oppression of the enemy?' As a shattering of my bones, my adversaries revile me, While they say to me all day long, 'Where is your God?' Why are you in despair, O my soul? And why have you become disturbed within me?" (vv. 9–11).

God was his rock, the thing he could count on no matter what. But now it seems as if the Rock had forgotten him. And it brings him depression and despair. He is mourning not only the loss of fellowship with God but that in its place have come trouble and trials. He knows God, but he doesn't know where God is. Does that sound familiar?

When Bible Verses Are Not Enough

The late Romanian minister Richard Wurmbrand spent fourteen years in a communist prison, during which time he was tortured repeatedly, one time spending three years in solitary confinement. He shared this:

> I've told the West how Christians were tied to crosses for four days and four nights. The crosses were put on the floor and other prisoners were tortured and made to fulfill their bodily necessities upon the faces and bodies of the crucified ones. I have since been asked "Which Bible verse helped and strengthened you in those circumstances?" My answer is, "No Bible verse was of any help. Bible verses alone are not meant to help." We knew Psalm 23. But when you pass through suffering you realize that it was never meant by God that Psalm 23 should strengthen you. It is the Lord who can strengthen you, not the psalm that speaks of Him doing so. It is not enough to have the psalm. You must have the One about whom the psalm speaks.[5]

The psalmist's enemies prompt him to say, "'Why do I go mourning because of the oppression of the enemy?' As a shattering of my bones, my adversaries revile me, while they say to me all day long, 'Where is your God?'" (vv. 9–10). The psalmist is telling God, "When they taunt me, Lord, they are really taunting You. They are taunting Your love and care for me. So now, at least for the moment, Lord, both my enemy and I have the same question: Why have You forgotten me?"

God allows us to vent what we feel even if it's not what we ultimately believe. The same psalmist who says, "Why have You forgotten me?" (v. 9) says in verse 11, "Hope in God, for I shall yet praise Him, the help of my countenance and my God." We know we can feel things we don't really believe.

Have you ever felt unappreciated, unloved? How many of us have felt as though God were going to allow our lives to go up in flames? How many times have we felt there was no hope that our situation would ever get better? And yet deep down we *know* there are people who love and appreciate us, that God won't allow our lives to go up in flames, and that there is still hope in God. But there are times when it doesn't feel that way.

Notice that God does not encourage dishonest prayers. You are free to share with Him what you are feeling at the moment (He knows it anyway), but there is something therapeutic in being able to vent your true feelings to your God. Feelings are how we react to sudden and discouraging circumstances. They are not truth or reality. They are merely an emotional response.

> There is something therapeutic in being able to vent your true feelings to your God.

In fact, what gives our faith such nobility and value to God is that we occasionally need to exercise it in direct opposition to what we are feeling at the moment. But He never requires us to deny what we are feeling. Isn't that refreshing to know? And don't you feel closer to those people you can be truly honest with? Maybe this is one of those things keeping you from drawing closer to God, the feeling that you can't be really honest with Him without Him getting mad at you.

Where Is Jesus in Psalm 42?

When we hear the words of the psalmist, we can't help but picture our Lord being ridiculed and mocked by His enemies. We read this in Matthew 27:41–43:

> In the same way the chief priests also, along with the scribes and elders, were mocking Him and saying, "He saved others; He cannot save Himself. He is the king of Israel; let Him now come down from the cross, and we will believe in Him. He trusts in God; let God rescue Him now, if He delights in Him."

Only a few verses later, Jesus cries out, "My God, My God, why have You forsaken Me?" (v. 46).

If you picture our Lord upon the cross and read this psalm through that lens, you will see so much that foreshadows His terrible suffering and agony on the cross. The Father had to turn His back on His Son—and what did that feel like? Read again the first part of Psalm 42. "My soul thirsts for God, for the living God; when shall I come and appear before God? My tears have been my food day and night, while they say to me all day long, 'Where is your God?'" (vv. 2–3).

And what about verse 7? "Deep calls to deep at the sound of Your waterfalls; all Your breakers and Your waves have rolled over me."

Jesus was overwhelmed by the flood of trouble, punishment, and despair He was experiencing. He was suffering for our sins. He was being overwhelmed by the punishment for all of us—it was cascading over Him like waves . . . Again, can you see Him in verses 9–10? "I will say to God my Rock, 'Why have You forgotten me? Why do I go mourning because of the oppression of the enemy?' As a shattering of my bones, my adversaries revile me, while they say to me all day long, 'Where is your God?'"

Yet where does our Lord eventually land? Read again verse 11: "Hope in God, for I shall yet praise Him." Jesus knew what was coming after the cross, after the suffering, after the darkness of the soul (Hebrews 12:2).

The anatomy of despair: too little God, too much stress. So the solution is more God, more Jesus, more faith in the face of powerful emotions and fears. There will be times when you will be overwhelmed with trouble, and you can't fix it. You just can't. You will need to ask God to do something for you that you can't do for yourself. Can you ask Him, "Fix this! I don't know how, but please fix this!" God answers that prayer every time, and always for our good. Not always instantly, but always. He will lead us safely out of every tunnel experience back into light.

And if you don't know Christ as your Savior, there is no solution to your despair apart from Him. You don't need more of Him—you need *Him*. You need a relationship with the God who made you, who loves you, who died for you. He is actually the thing you have been wanting all along, the only thing that can satisfy the deepest longings of your heart.

QUESTIONS

1. What is something (or several things) that is really stressing you right now? Name them, and explain why they are so difficult for you. What is the underlying fear behind the stress?

2. Have you experienced that feeling, or yearning, for something you can't quite put your finger on? What other things do people often try to fill that need with? Can you think of something, or some activity, that you have been trying to use to fill that space that only God can fill in your life? If so, what is it?

3. Think about some experiences in your life that have stolen your happiness. As you look back upon them, how many were tunnels you eventually came out of? How did God help you? What did He do to bring back your joy or happiness? How might that affect your faith in God in the current tunnel you are in?

4. Charles Swindoll talks about our "churning place." How do you respond physically and emotionally to problems and stresses in your life? How do they display in your life?

Chapter Ten

Returning to God . . .
from a Long Way Off

Psalm 51

Thomas Tarrants grew up in a Baptist church to a dear Baptist mother, attending church regularly. He knew hell was a terrible reality and didn't want to go there when he died. He made a profession of faith when he was thirteen and was baptized, but he eventually realized the decision had been motivated not by faith but by fear.

Thomas grew up in the South in the midst of the civil rights of the 1960s. He was deeply patriotic and wanted to serve God and his country. For him, however, it eventually meant embracing far-right extremism, with its hatred of Blacks, Jews, communists, socialists, and liberals.

He eventually got involved with Mississippi's dreaded White Knights of the Ku Klux Klan, the most violent terrorist organization at the time in the United States. He was so entrenched in its ideology that he and an accomplice attempted to plant a bomb at the home of a Jewish businessman in Meridian, Mississippi. But they were ambushed in a police stakeout. He was critically wounded by a shotgun blast at close range. His survival was a miracle.

After recovering, Thomas was sent to the Mississippi State Penitentiary, one of the worst prisons in America. Six months later he escaped, intending to continue his terrorism. A few days later, however, he was apprehended in a blazing gun battle with the authorities. He was then confined to a six-by-nine-foot cell in the maximum-security section. To keep from going crazy, he read voraciously. He began by reading more racist and anti-Semitic literature.

But seeking truth, he also read classical philosophy and eventually the New Testament, specifically the Gospels. And as he did, his eyes were opened in a new way to the truth he had learned as a child. And then his sins came to his mind, one after another, and conviction grew within him. Thomas cried tears of repentance and sought Christ's forgiveness, kneeling on the floor of his cell and asking Christ to forgive his sins and take over his life—and do whatever He wanted to do with it.

As Thomas read the Bible now, a new world opened up to him. His hate died away, and he made friends with Black inmates and others who were different from him—including the FBI agent who had orchestrated his capture and the Jewish lawyer who helped him. He served eight years in prison.

He was paroled and entered a university, which led him ultimately to campus ministry, pastoral ministry in a racially mixed church, and finally to a long ministry of teaching, discipling, spiritual mentoring, and writing at the C. S. Lewis Institute, where Thomas became president emeritus of the institute and the author of *Consumed by Hate, Redeemed by Love: How a Violent Klansman Became a Champion of Racial Reconciliation.*[1]

Psalm 51 is written by David and refers to the time in his life when he was a long way off from God and wanted desperately to return to him. Like Thomas Tarrants, David's sin had derailed his spiritual life. Was there a way back? Maybe that's you. Maybe you feel a long way off from God and want to return. David is going to show us that returning to God . . .

Starts with Confession

We often think, when we have offended God, that the first thing we need to do is something good, to change our behavior. But David shows that something else must come first:

Be gracious to me, O God, according to Your lovingkindness; according to the greatness of Your compassion blot out my transgressions. Wash me thoroughly from my iniquity and cleanse me from my sin. For I know my transgressions, and my sin is ever before me. Against You, You only, I have sinned and done what is evil in Your sight, so that You are justified when You speak and blameless when You judge.

Behold, I was brought forth in iniquity, and in sin my mother conceived me. Behold, You desire truth in the innermost being, and in the hidden part You will make me know wisdom. (vv. 1–6)

The background to this psalm is explained as, "When Nathan the prophet came to him after he had gone in to Bathsheba." King David had seen a beautiful married woman bathing, desired her sexually, and sent for her. He then slept with her, and she got pregnant. When he learned of her pregnancy, he tried every way he could to hide the sin, to the point of having her husband, one of his loyal soldiers, murdered. This was the sin that had derailed David's life and to which he refers in this psalm.

Don't miss this—David enshrines his sin for the ages. How would you like your sin enshrined for the ages? So what does David ask for? He asks God to "be gracious . . . according to Your lovingkindness" (v. 1). And God *had* been gracious to David—by exposing his sin through Nathan the prophet. Unconfessed sin would have ruined David. His sinful activity would have grown worse—his character, his values would have been forever scarred. One of the most gracious things God does is expose the sin we try to hide. He wants to bring healing. Hiding it brings ruin.

To be *gracious* is to ask God to give you something you don't deserve. But the word *lovingkindness* is a covenant word, a word that described God's attitude toward His people Israel, and precisely what David needed now. He appeals to a prior relationship, the way things used to be. In the parable of the prodigal son in the New Testament, when the prodigal returns home, he is hoping only to be one of his father's servants. But when his father arrives, the prodigal son says, "Father, I have sinned against heaven and in your sight; I am no longer worthy to be called your son" (Luke 15:21).

Though the son realizes he has sinned against his father greatly, he still calls him father. He knew who to return to—where he would get the best treatment.

Returning is what Psalm 51 is all about. In both sin and obedience there is embracing and turning away. Either we embrace sin and turn away from God, or we embrace God and turn away from sin. David continues, "According to the greatness of Your compassion blot out my transgressions. Wash me thoroughly from my iniquity and cleanse me from my sin" (vv. 1–2).

David understands that he can't undo what he has done. His sin clings to him like a tattoo. He needs to be "washed." This Hebrew verb was used for laundering clothes. David knows that the stain of his sin is deep in his heart and soul and it will take a lot to clean it out.

If you talk with Annette, she will tell you that I have a disturbing and frequent habit of spilling food on myself. Most often on my shirt. I drop all kinds of foods on my shirts—especially ice cream. You'd think with a mouth as big as mine, I'd hit the target more. But recently I stained my shirt with some sauce that was stubborn. We put special cleansers on it, but it didn't go away. So she tried washing it again and putting more special cleansers on it. It is faded but still there. Some stains go deeper and require deeper cleaning. David understood that.

There is a stain on David's heart and soul that is indelible. Nothing he can do can remove it. Only God can remove this stain. David begs God to do just this. He wants more than anything else to be cleansed from "my sin." David knows that though he had sinned against Bathsheba, Uriah, and Israel, only God can remove his guilt. Even if they all forgive him, he still needs God to forgive him. His sins are still on his mind.

Do you have such a sin, a sin so bad in your mind God could never forgive you? Has it been on your mind for a long time? Do you say with David, "For I know my transgressions, and my sin is ever before me" (v. 3)?

We are continually told that morality is a human creation—and so, therefore, is the idea of sin. There is no real right and wrong, just what's right and wrong for you. If that is true, there is certainly no need for a Savior or forgiveness or cleansing from sin.

Yet we live in a world that drugs itself and counsels itself continually to try to deal with the inner unhappiness and dread and guilt we can't seem to escape. We were made in the image of God, and the residue of that image reacts badly to sin. It will always be so. Our conscience senses our sin even when we try to deny it or explain it away. The path to freedom is not to rationalize sin away but to confess it and seek forgiveness and cleansing. And that begins by calling sin what it is.

> The path to freedom is not to rationalize sin away but to confess it and seek forgiveness and cleansing.

"For I know my transgressions, and my sin is ever before me." "I lied." "I am bitter." "I am angry." "I am dishonest." "I am jealous." "I am resentful." "I lust." "I committed adultery." "I committed murder." "I was unfaithful." "I was cruel." We need to call sin, sin. Then David goes on, "Against You, You only, I have sinned and done what is evil in Your sight, so that You are justified when You speak and blameless when You judge" (v. 4).

Now David isn't saying that he didn't sin against Bathsheba and Uriah and Israel, but he recognizes that it was God's law he broke by doing so, not Bathsheba's or Uriah's. He had an even greater responsibility to God than to Uriah or Bathsheba.

Sin is treason against God. If you try to overthrow the government, and in the process, you harm or murder someone, you will still be tried for treason because you have betrayed the country you confessed allegiance to.

Every sin is cosmic treason, trying to overthrow the rule of the One to whom you owe everything. In 2 Samuel 11, David was only trying to cover his tracks, hide his sin. The idea was, "How can I cover this up?" Yet now we see David answering a different question. "How could I have done this to God, who has given me so much?" Ironically, in sin, we are often chasing something God wants for us—yet in the wrong way. In a letter to a lifelong friend, Arthur Greeves, C. S. Lewis wrote about this. He used the illustration of his dog.

> Supposing you are taking a dog on a lead . . . past a post. You know what happens. . . . He tries to go on the wrong side and gets his head looped round the post. *You see* that he can't do it. . . . You pull *back* because you want to enable him to go *forward*. He wants exactly the same thing—namely to go *forward*; for that very reason he resists

your pull *back*, . . . though *in fact* it is only by yielding to you that he will ever succeed in getting where he wants.

Later in the letter, Lewis shared what he would tell his dog—who wanted his own will—if he could.

My dear dog, if by your will you mean what you really want to do, viz. to get forward along the road, I not only understand this desire but *share* it. . . .

If by your will, on the other hand, you mean your will to pull against the collar and try to force yourself forward in a direction which is no use—why I understand it of course, but just because I understand it . . . I cannot possibly share it.[2]

Lewis goes on to explain that God both understands and created our desires for ecstatic joy and overwhelming happiness. But we, like the dog, try to attain this in ways that will only take us further from it. God knows, and I do not, how to attain this.

David desires ecstatic joy and overwhelming happiness, but he does not know how to attain this. He admits to God that "You are justified when You speak and blameless when You judge. Behold, I was brought forth in iniquity, and in sin my mother conceived me. Behold, You desire truth in the innermost being, and in the hidden part You will make me know wisdom" (vv. 4–6).

Bathsheba and Uriah could definitely accuse David of sin—but they were also guilty of sins. Sometimes, if you point out someone's sin to them, they reply, "So you're perfect? You've never done anything wrong? People who live in glass houses shouldn't throw rocks." It's an attempt to redirect guilt away from themselves. But you can't do that with God. He *is* perfect. He *is* without sin. When He accuses someone of sin, He does so without embarrassment that He might also be accused of some evil.

David also understands that he did not become evil by this act but that he was born that way. We don't *become* sinful when we sin—we sin because we *are* sinful. Our sin is a reflection of our true heart, which is why it's so easy to be cruel, proud, thoughtless, angry, jealous, bitter, lustful, or greedy, and why it's so hard to be unselfish, kind, patient, understanding, and sacrificial toward others. It's why we don't have to teach our children to do the wrong thing. It's instinctual. We spend our lives trying to teach them to do the right thing—because it's so unnatural.

Returning to God from a long way off begins with confessing to God—being honest about your sin. Knowing that God demands you be self-honest, that He desires "truth in the innermost being." Without this step, there can simply be nothing else. But once you confess, returning to God then . . .

Moves to Restoration

To be restored, God must do things in us and for us, and we must trust Him to do them. And we must *invite* them, not *resist* them. So David writes,

> Purify me with hyssop, and I shall be clean; wash me, and I shall be whiter than snow. Make me to hear joy and gladness, let the bones which You have broken rejoice. Hide Your face from my sins and blot out all my iniquities.
>
> Create in me a clean heart, O God, and renew a steadfast spirit within me. Do not cast me away from Your presence and do not take Your Holy Spirit from me. Restore to me the joy of Your salvation and sustain me with a willing spirit. Then I will teach transgressors Your ways, and sinners will be converted to You. (vv. 7–13)

Do we speak to God this way? Do we dare? We need to if we are to be honest with God.

Hyssop was a plant or bush, the branches of which were used in ceremonies to apply sacrificial blood. The Hebrews used hyssop to apply the blood to the lintels of their doors in Egypt before the angel of death passed by. In Leviticus 14:1–4 we read that when a leper had been healed, if he was sprinkled seven times with the sacrificial blood, they could then be pronounced clean. This is what David is referring to. If God could work the miracle of cleansing a leper of leprosy, He could cleanse a sinner of his or her sin—which was equally a miracle.

How does a person remove the stain of personal guilt? It's invisible but so very real. In Tim Keller's book *The Prodigal Prophet*, he wrote,

Adam and Eve did not say, "Let's be evil. Let's ruin our own lives, and everyone else's too!" Rather, they thought, "We just want to be happy. But His commands don't look like they will give us the things that we need to thrive. We will have to take things into our own hands—we can't trust Him." . . . Sin always begins with the character assassination of God. We believe that God has put us in a world of delights but has determined that He will not give them to us if we obey Him." . . . The Serpent told the human race that disobeying God was the only way to realize their fullest happiness and potential, and this delusion has sunk deep into every human heart.[3]

It is this belief, this idea, that must also be washed from us in order for us to be restored, or we will only be restored . . . to sin again. So David writes, "Make me to hear joy and gladness, let the bones which You have broken rejoice. Hide Your face from my sins and blot out all my iniquities." Like C. S. Lewis's dog example, we need to say, "I trust that the way You are leading me is really the best way, and I will be not only *compliant* but *eager* to follow You the way You lead.

"I want to experience the joy You have for me; I want to experience gladness again. I want to have the 'bones which You have broken rejoice,' meaning, I want to feel whole again. I want You to 'Hide Your face from my sins.' I don't want You looking at me through the lens of my greatest mistake for the rest of my life. 'Create in me a clean heart, O God, and renew a steadfast spirit within me.'"

What an incredibly important prayer to pray to God.

Create it! It's not there now. Even when things are bad, we can all have moments when we go to a party, celebrate something, and feel temporary reprieve. But then the darkness of guilt and sorrow return. We want to be a new person, and we want the newness to last, "renew a steadfast spirit." Only God can promise you this—and only God can deliver on this promise. He has done it in life after life. Including my own.

But have we asked God for this? To ask God for help in this area of life is to admit your weakness and need of His help.

Do not cast me away from Your presence and do not take Your Holy Spirit from me. Restore to me the joy of Your salvation and sustain

me with a willing spirit. Then I will teach transgressors Your ways,
and sinners will be converted to You. (vv. 11–13)

David had seen the Spirit of God be removed from Saul and the dread that caused in the king's life. He didn't want that. In the Old Testament, the Spirit of God came upon people but didn't abide in them as He does within believers today.

David promises that if God will restore the joy of his salvation, he will "teach transgressors Your ways . . . sinners will be converted to You." Why? we might ask. It's because they will see how God responds to our failures when we truly repent. Realizing how you will be received when you have failed spectacularly determines whether you feel safe admitting your failures to God, and asking for Him to restore you.

So returning to God starts with confession, moves to restoration, and finally . . .

Ends in Deliverance

If you have been rescued from the ocean's waves by a lifeguard, the experience you most want is to plant your feet firmly upon the sand again, where the waves can no longer threaten you. That's the end game. The end game in repentance before God is to be finally and completely delivered. So we read David praying,

Deliver me from bloodguiltiness, O God, the God of my salvation;
then my tongue will joyfully sing of Your righteousness. O Lord,
open my lips, that my mouth may declare Your praise. For You do not
delight in sacrifice, otherwise I would give it; You are not pleased with
burnt offering. The sacrifices of God are a broken spirit; a broken
and a contrite heart, O God, You will not despise. By Your favor do
good to Zion; build the walls of Jerusalem. Then You will delight in
righteous sacrifices, in burnt offering and whole burnt offering; then
young bulls will be offered on Your altar. (vv. 14–19)

David has blood on his hands. He'd murdered Uriah. He could never wipe this away. And yet David realizes that God is "the God of my salvation." He is the actual rescuer. He sees his deliverance before it comes because he had come to know by experience the heart and character of God. He knows that soon "my tongue will joyfully sing of Your righteousness. O Lord, open my lips, that my mouth may declare Your praise" (vv. 14–15). Then David utters something that is confusing to some. "For You do not delight in sacrifice, otherwise I would give it; You are not pleased with burnt offering. The sacrifices of God are a broken spirit; a broken and a contrite heart, O God, You will not despise" (vv. 16–17).

What God is waiting for is the heart that says, "I'm sinful and I'm helpless against it—and I desperately need Your help, God. I don't want to live like this anymore." David is not dissing the sacrifices God required of His people but seeing the deeper truth there. It is tempting to think, Oh, I've blown it with God, but no problem. I'll just dash off some sacrifices, burn a few offerings, and start attending church more regularly for a while, and everything will be hunky-dory. People do the same thing today.

"I've done bad things, so I will just do some good things to make up for them. That way I can look God in the eye." But as I've shared before, that is faulty thinking. Good deeds do not cancel out bad ones. Good deeds are good to do, don't misunderstand me, but they do not *undo* even one bad deed. That's why we put people in prison instead of giving them coupon books of good things to do to pay for their bad deeds.

Sacrifices and offerings point to a deep truth—someone else is paying for your sin. An innocent lamb, bull, goat, dove is taking the punishment you deserve. God doesn't want people treating those offerings and sacrifices frivolously like get-out-of-jail-free cards. God is looking, as Dr. Derek Kidner writes, "for the heart that knows how little it deserves, and how much it owes."[4] What God really wants is a heart that is truly broken over sin. Then David says, "By Your favor do good to Zion; build the walls of Jerusalem. Then You will delight in righteous sacrifices, in burnt offering and whole burnt offering; then young bulls will be offered on Your altar" (vv. 18–19).

It's very possible that these words were not written by David but added later by future generations who lived between the exile of Israel and the return to their homeland—to help identify with the idea of being restored to God's good graces.

It was only another example of how, even though Israel as a nation had disobeyed God, and He had to punish them by allowing them to be conquered and exiled, yet as they repented and turned back to Him, He restored them by mercy and grace.

This is what God wants to bring to the life of all who have sinned. Deliverance. The way to return to God from a long way off starts with confession, moves to restoration, and ends in deliverance. Only one of those steps is ours. *Confession*. God does the rest!

Where Is Jesus in Psalm 51?

In verses 1 and 9 we read David asking God to "blot out my transgressions . . . blot out all my iniquities." This literally means to wipe the writing out of a book. The first time we sin, we create a record, the same way a person who is arrested suddenly gets a record. Something is on the books against me. A prisoner can do his or her time and get that record expunged, but how do we expunge our guilt against God? The penalty for sin is eternal death!

Through the Spirit, David is looking forward to something that is only fully revealed in the New Testament. The answer is Jesus. Paul tells the Corinthians that "He made Him who knew no sin to be sin on our behalf, so that we might become the righteousness of God in Him" (2 Corinthians 5:21). And Paul tells the Colossians what God has done for us, "Having canceled out the certificate of debt consisting of decrees against us, which was hostile to us, and He has taken it out of the way, having nailed it to the cross" (Colossians 2:14).

God can hide His face from our sins precisely because He once hid His face from Jesus on the cross as He was punished for our sins. Jesus took our sins out of the way, removed them. So now we can return to God . . . from a long way off.

Are you ready to return to God? Are you ready to talk honestly and genuinely about your sin? As Christians we can do so with great assurance because we have an advocate with the Father—the Son, Jesus Christ. Are you tired of the spiritual and emotional distance between you and God? Tell Him. Be honest with God.

It's what He's been waiting for.

QUESTIONS

1. Can you recall a time when you were a long way off from God because of some sin in your life? How had that sin derailed your spiritual walk with God? Why do you think it was so hard to return to Him?

2. David didn't want God looking at him through the lens of his greatest mistake for the rest of his life. So he asked God to "hide Your face from my sins." Have you asked God to create a new heart within you, even as you are struggling with your sin? Tell God how you desperately want your relationship with Him to be joyful again. Be honest!

3. David was willing to be used of God to teach transgressors God's way, as a result of how God had taught him. Can you think of a time when you were able to give someone counsel as a result of how God disciplined you? What did you tell them?

Chapter Eleven

Bridging Our Distance from God

Psalm 53

One of Annette's and my favorite movies is *Bridge of Spies*, starring Tom Hanks. We love it because it's a true story of a riveting historical event that took place during the Cold War between America and Russia in the 1960s. Tom Hanks plays attorney James Donovan, who is hired to represent a Russian spy named Rudolph Abel in court. He does so, and well enough that while Abel is convicted, his life is spared.

Later, an American pilot flying a U-2 spy plane over Russia was shot down. Now each side had a spy they wanted back. This would lead to a trip by Donovan to East Berlin to try to broker the deal. East and West Berlin were the separate parts of two competing political systems. East Berlin, controlled by the Russians, was sterile, barren, bombed out, and under tyranny. West Berlin was vibrant, prosperous, and free.

Separating the two parts of the city ran the Havel River. Spanning both sides was the Glienicke Bridge. The bridge spanned not only two cities but two different ways of life. One life was free, the other was not. The Glienicke Bridge later became known as the Bridge of Spies, as a number of prisoner exchanges were made on it.

This bridge was important to two prisoners. Hope didn't seem to exist for either of them. It seemed as if they would spend many years in prison—or worse. For each prisoner, their life on the side of the river they were on spelled only prison and hopelessness. On the other side of the river lay freedom. Their only hope was to cross the Glienicke Bridge.

Both men were guilty of what they had been sentenced for. Yet both men were putting their hope for freedom in crossing Glienicke Bridge on February 10, 1962, and a prisoner exchange. Both of them ultimately did. And this brings us to Psalm 53, which speaks of the great distance between a holy God and an unholy people—and yet ends with the great hope of a bridge and a prisoner exchange!

We will see in Psalm 53 that we need desperately to understand . . .

The Distance between Us and God

If you were to ask average persons on the street the question "What do you think God thinks of you right now?" you would probably get different responses. But most of the responses would likely be along these lines: "Well, he/she/it knows I'm not perfect, but that I try pretty hard and am generally a really good person." Most people would be astonished to find God *doesn't* think that. David understands what God sees when He looks down at man. So he writes,

For the choir director; according to Mahalath. A Maskil of David.

The fool has said in his heart, "There is no God," they are corrupt, and have committed abominable injustice; there is no one who does good. God has looked down from heaven upon the sons of men to see if there is anyone who understands, who seeks after God. Every one of them has turned aside; together they have become corrupt; there is no one who does good, not even one. (vv. 1–3)

Mahalath could be the name of a tone or an instrument. It is almost identical with the word for sickness, which is why the New American Standard Bible describes it as "a sad tone." The idea could be that this is a sad teaching, a tragic but necessary truth, a somber psalm.

Psalm 14 and Psalm 53 are virtually identical until verses 5 and 6. Psalm 14 is a warning to unbelievers to fear because God really exists. Psalm 53 is a call to believers. Since God has already defeated their enemies, why are they filled with dread? David begins pulling no punches: "The fool has said in his heart, 'There is no God.'"

Without apology David claims it is the height of folly to claim there is no God. There is no justification, no excuse for that belief. God has not left us without overwhelming evidence. The last word on atheism is found in Romans 1:22: "Professing to be wise, they became fools." In Romans 1:19 Paul explained it is "because that which is known about God is evident within them; for God made it evident to them." And in verse 28 he wrote, "And just as they did not see fit to acknowledge God any longer, God gave them over to a depraved mind, to do those things which are not proper."

The Hebrew word for fool, *nabal*, is a word that suggests an aggressive perversity.[1] There was a character in Scripture with the name Nabal in 1 Samuel. He was Abigail's husband, who had enjoyed protection from David's men from enemies around him but then treated David shamefully. David was soon on his way to dole out punishment. But Abigail intercepted David and told him, "Please do not let my lord pay attention to this worthless man, Nabal, for as his name is, so is he. Nabal is his name and folly is with him" (1 Samuel 25:25).

To protect her husband, she had to admit that he was rightly named. In fact, he lived up to his name beautifully—he was a complete fool. There are many words for *fool* in Hebrew. But one commentator reminds us that a *nabal* is a species of fool, base and worthless, and an object of scorn. He is never merely stupid but morally deficient.[2]

We are told in Proverbs 1:7 that "the fear of the LORD is the beginning of knowledge." The flip side of that is "the fool has said in his heart, there is no God." When you deny the reality of God, that begins the slide into folly. Behind every sin lurks the idea that there is no God.

Defiance of God

In an article speaking of why six women became satanists, they explain that "Satanism is an atheist belief system, which engages with Satan not as a genuine demonic being or evil presence, but as an icon of rebellion. . . . 'Satan is a symbol of intellectual freedom and rebellion against tyranny.'"[3] What tyranny are they rebelling against? They are rebelling against God, who would claim their obedience and hold them accountable.

Interestingly, the statement "there is no God" in the Bible is never treated simply as a misguided conviction but as *defiance*. In Psalm 10:4 we read, "The wicked, in the haughtiness of his countenance, does not seek Him. All his thoughts are, 'There is no God.'" Job described those who are wicked and said of them, "They say to God, 'Depart from us.' We do not even desire the knowledge of Your ways. Who is the Almighty, that we should serve Him, and what would we gain if we entreat Him?" (Job 21:14–15).

Not everyone behaves as arrogantly about their atheism as others, though. Some cannot believe in God but have no animosity toward those who do. But they are not acting wisely from God's perspective.

Everyone seems to believe in their heart of hearts that they know more than God what is best, what is true, what is wise. They feel they don't have the "God need" other weaker or less intelligent people have. David continues, "They are corrupt, and have committed abominable injustice; there is no one who does good."

It is instructive to note that God is surprised and disappointed that in all of humanity, not one person truly does good. Why the surprise and disappointment? It's because we were made in the image of God (Genesis 1:26–27). And yet with that enormous advantage, not one person truly seeks Him. Sadly, the acorn did not fall anywhere near the tree.

As Isaiah said, "All of us like sheep have gone astray; each of us has turned to his own way" (Isaiah 53:6). In our world we talk about people who are seeking God. Yet God claims that no one actually does. How do we reconcile these two ideas? Simply this: no one is seeking the *true* God, the *real* one. That's Paul's point in Romans 1:22–23, 25: "Professing to be wise, they became fools, and exchanged the glory of the incorruptible God for an image in the form of corruptible man and of birds and four-footed animals and crawling creatures. . . . For they exchanged the truth of God for a lie, and worshipped and served the creature rather than the Creator, who is blessed forever."

Designer Gods

We want our own designer gods, gods that we can create and control and that will flatter us. So rather than seeking God, everyone is actually running away from the real God. It's why Jesus had to come to seek us. As He said, "For the Son of Man has come to seek and to save that which was lost" (Luke 19:10). God has to seek us because we *aren't* seeking Him. David continues, "God has looked down from heaven upon the sons of men to see if there is anyone who understands, who seeks after God. Every one of them has turned aside; together they have become corrupt; there is no one who does good, not even one."

For those who have read the Scriptures a lot, these words will sound familiar. Paul quoted them in Romans 3:10–12. When Paul wanted to explain the problem of the human heart and its alienation from God, he went to Psalm 53 and Psalm 14. No one was seeking God in the Old Testament, no one was seeking God in the New Testament, and no one is seeking the true God today.

It's like the person who says they are looking for a job. But after a long time has gone by, they still can't seem to find employment. You tell them about an open position. But they say, "No, I don't want that job," and proceed to tell you why. So you keep looking. But every job you tell them about, you get the same response: "No, I don't want that job." Eventually you realize they don't really want a job. They enjoy not working, but they want you to think they are serious about their job search.

In the same way there are people who say they are looking for God, but when you tell them about God, they say, "Oh no, I don't want *that* kind of a god." The problem is that God is the only one there is whether you like it or not. And what keeps us from wanting the true God is the sin within us. And sin is a real thing.

Aleksandr Solzhenitsyn was imprisoned in a Russian prison camp and endured terrible treatment but learned so much there. In *The Gulag Archipelago*, he wrote, "Gradually it was disclosed to me that the line separating good and evil passes not through states, nor between classes, nor between political parties either—but right through every human heart—and through all human hearts."[4] Paul said it simply in Romans 3:23, "For all have sinned and fall short of the glory of God." All, not just most. All.

David is reminding us of the moral and spiritual distance between us and God. There are times when our prayers involve insight we have gained from our walk with God. We share these truths in prayer because we realize we needed His wisdom to overcome our innate foolishness and rebellion. Such wisdom is something not only to be grateful for but to praise Him for.

When we do this, we are echoing His great work in our hearts and minds. Do you share with God what great wisdom He has revealed to you in His Word? This blesses our God. And it is healthy for us spiritually.

But the somber psalm continues with seeing . . .

The Tragic Way Life Ends without God

The same story occurs every day, as it has for all of history's past. Those who rebel against God have only one destiny, one way their life can end without Christ. So David writes,

> Have the workers of wickedness no knowledge, who eat up My people as though they ate bread and have not called upon God? There they were in great fear where no fear had been; for God scattered the bones of him who encamped against you; you put them to shame, because God had rejected them. (vv. 4–5)

Because of the foolish belief there is no God, the hostile atheist or agnostic may feel safe in persecuting, mocking, and even trying to remove the faithful from the community. They reason logically: if there is no God, then there is no God to protect His people—and we can treat them any way we like. Since their views make us uncomfortable, we need to find a way to banish them from the marketplace of ideas.

So, as David says, they feel free to "eat up My people as though they ate bread" (v. 4). They feel free to do whatever they want to God's people, including removing from them the necessaries of life. Often, when the church is persecuted, the first thing that happens is people feel free to take their possessions. And this happens in any persecution. Didn't it happen to the Jews in World War II? When they had been deemed "unacceptable," people felt free to take what was theirs. And they had no fear in doing so.

Recently, some friends who are missionaries sent an amazing testimony from the team in the field. It read:

> Our staff team went to a church and met a 16-year-old girl named Brina (not her real name), who recognized one of the girls on the

team as the one who had given her a Bible two years earlier. The girl on our team hadn't thought much of it at the time, as Brina was 14 years old at the time, and they hadn't had much time together.

As Brina shared her testimony, we heard how she took that Bible back to her village, and while reading Matthew 6, was struck by the Lord's Prayer and later where Jesus said, "Look at the birds of the air; they neither sow nor reap, nor gather into barns, and yet your Heavenly Father feeds them. Are you not more precious than they?" Right then she was converted and gave her life to Christ. She then delivered two people of demons, including her own brother. Her family, until then, had been . . . oppressed by demons, and the father would go into trances and say that he'd eat his kids, and lots of other terrible things.

Brina bravely witnessed to her family and over a couple of weeks led her whole family to the Lord! Beyond that, a further 16 people have been led to the Lord in their area by this 16-year-old and her 14-year-old brother. Their village persecuted them mercilessly. They couldn't even drink water from the village well or eat in anyone's home. Later, their neighbors drove them out of the village, and they are now living in the main town of the district. On top of this, their father was terribly injured in an accident, and since the kids are in school the mother works carrying manure to other people's farms to provide for the family. Despite all these difficulties, the family is filled with joy and can't stop talking about Jesus with everyone they meet.[5]

But we don't read that God's people are abandoned and terrified—we read what God will do to the enemies of His people. "There they were in great fear where no fear had been; for God scattered the bones of him who encamped against you; you put them to shame, because God had rejected them" (v. 5).

He filled their enemies with fear! Verse 1 shows the fool having no fear of God, no reason to believe God would ever intercede in his private life. But now God produces the very fear the unbeliever tries to avoid. In 2 Kings 7:6, we read of the army of the Arameans coming against Israel and that the Hebrews were in great danger. But God caused the Arameans to hear the sounds of a great army, and they assumed it was hired armies of the Hittites and Egyptians coming, and they dropped everything and ran away. All out of fear.

God does not need an army to defeat one. He simply uses fear. As we would say, "They were afraid of shadows!" God knows what it will take to get our attention. God often uses storms to wake us up to dangers that will ruin our lives if we don't change course. God wants to save us, He wants to rescue us, but when we are hell-bent on ignoring Him, He will do painful things to get our attention.

Sticks and Stones of Love

In his book *The Prodigal Prophet,* pastor Tim Keller recalled a fairy tale he had read years ago:

[It was] about a wicked witch who lived in a remote cottage in the deep forest. When travelers came through looking for lodging, she offered them a meal and a bed. It was the most wonderfully comfortable bed any of them had ever felt. But it was a bed full of dark magic, and if you were asleep in it when the sun came up, you would turn to stone. Then you became a figure in the witch's statuary, trapped until the end of time. This witch forced a young girl to serve her, and though she had no power to resist the witch, the girl had become more and more filled with pity for her victims.

One day a young man came looking for bed and board and was taken in. The servant girl could not bear to see him turned to stone. So she threw sticks, stones, and thistles into his bed. It made the bed horribly uncomfortable. Every time he turned he felt a new painful object under him. Though he cast each one out, there was always a new one to dig into his flesh. He slept only fitfully and finally rose, feeling weary and worn, long before dawn. As he walked out the front door, the servant girl met him, and he berated her cruelly. "How could you give a traveler such a terrible bed full of sticks and stones?" he cried and went on his way. "Ah," she said under her breath, "the misery you know now is nothing like the infinitely greater misery a comfortable sleep would have brought upon you! Those were my sticks and stones of love."[6]

This psalm speaks here of judgment! Fear! Shame! That's what awaits the person who ultimately rejects God. Why? Because when you reject God, you make it necessary for Him to reject you. "Because God had rejected them."

You cannot continually deny and reject God and then expect He will ignore it and not deal with it. There is an eternal price in hell to be paid for rejecting God. But the Bible is the story of God's offer of grace!

What does the Bible teach about God's people? Because of what Jesus has done, we read in Romans 15:7, "Therefore, accept one another, just as Christ also accepted us to the glory of God."

The person without Christ has no one to rescue them at the end. The people of God do. So to bridge our distance from God, we need to see the distance between us and God and the tragic way life ends without God.

There are times in prayer when God's Spirit brings to our minds examples of how He has blessed us and how He has dealt with our enemies. When we remember these events and see the end of the wicked, we are moved to pray for them, as Jesus did.

Communicating our sadness to God over the plight of those who rebel against Him is part of our developing conversation with God. We articulate in our prayers the very heart of God and feel as He feels. Honesty begets a deeper level of relationship.

Life can end tragically without God, yet there is hope! We need to see finally . . . the Bridge of hope God created.

And here we see so beautifully, so wonderfully . . .

Where Is Jesus in Psalm 53?

"Oh, that the salvation of Israel would come out of Zion! When God restores His captive people, let Jacob rejoice, let Israel be glad."

God decided to bridge the awful distance between Himself and sinful man by sending us a Savior—Himself! What is the ultimate answer to the ones who deny God and persecute the ungodly? The coming of the Messiah! David longs for the coming Messiah to arrive and rescue once and for all His people. On that day Jacob and Israel would rejoice!

David echoes the longing of God's people of all ages. The battle against God and His people continues, and we get weary of it. We are anxious for it to just stop. What David didn't know was that when Messiah first came, it would be to deliver all captive people from the greatest danger they face—eternal punishment. They needed to be rescued from sin and the punishment it deserved.

God would first restore the hearts of the people by His death and resurrection and the promise of new life in Him. Later, when He comes again—He will come as King of kings and end all rebellion for all time. And He will usher in eternal peace for the people of God.

God *did* come out of Zion and restore captives. Paul, speaking to the Ephesian Christians, wrote about Jesus that "When He ascended on high, He led captive a host of captives, and He gave gifts to men" (Ephesians 4:8).

We read in Luke of Jesus taking the book of Isaiah. "And the book of the prophet Isaiah was handed to Him. And He opened the book and found the place where it was written, 'The Spirit of the LORD is upon Me, because He anointed Me to preach the gospel to the poor. He has sent Me to proclaim release to the captives'" (Luke 4:17–18).

People tend to roll their eyes when you start saying stuff like this. They point out that the real problems of the world are war, violence, prejudice, poverty, and abuse, while the church dabbles in solving the problems of sin. But sin is what causes the wars, violence, prejudice, poverty, and abuse. It's what's inside of man that is causing all those problems. That's where the solution lies. Change the heart of man and you will change all those other things.

There will come a day when Christ will come again in judgment upon the world and put down all rebellions against Him. But the rescue David longed for has already begun. We have been immunized against eternal death and God's judgment upon sin by the blood of Jesus. Yet we walk among people who have not been immunized, in the hopes we can persuade them to yet be immunized.

> We have been immunized against eternal death and God's judgment upon sin by the blood of Jesus.

We will all catch the symptoms of death, as when we are vaccinated many experience symptoms of the very flu they are being vaccinated against. But when the symptom of death touches the believer, by accident, illness, disease, depression, or something else, and our physical body dies, death must immediately release them, and we instantly enter the presence of God. Why? We have been immunized with the blood of Jesus!

John Stott, in his book *The Cross of Christ*, wrote,

> The biblical gospel of atonement is of God satisfying Himself by substituting Himself for us. The concept of substitution may be said, then, to lie at the heart of both sin and salvation. For the essence of sin is man substituting himself for God, while the essence of salvation is God substituting Himself for man. Man asserts himself against God and puts himself where only God deserves to be; God sacrifices Himself for man and puts Himself where only man deserves to be. Man claims prerogatives which belong to God alone; God accepts penalties which belong to man alone.[7]

"For the wages of sin is death, but the free gift of God is eternal life in Christ Jesus our Lord" (Romans 6:23). Jesus is the bridge between the holy God and an unholy people. All David could envision in this psalm was Israel's rescue from their human enemies, but the Holy Spirit was pointing forward to a much greater deliverance to come.

Our salvation is the result of a prisoner exchange, just like on the Glienicke Bridge. Jesus was exchanged for all of us. He was punished so we could all be free and escape punishment. But after Jesus's punishment, God raised Him from the dead, and a bridge was created that allowed any who wanted grace and mercy to cross over to Jesus and find eternal safety.

Salvation *did* come out of Zion! The Bridge is waiting for any who want to cross over. We who have crossed over should continually rejoice. God never tires of hearing our thanks and praise to Him for His rescue of us. Be honest to God about your feelings of thanks and gratitude. May our prayers become to Him a fragrant aroma.

QUESTIONS

1. An instructive question to ask ourselves from time to time is this: "What do you think God thinks of you right now?" Write down two or three sentences about what you feel God thinks of you right now, and why.

2. David writes, "The fool has said in his heart, 'There is no God.'" Has there ever been a time when this reflected your own thoughts? Why had you come to believe there was no God, and what caused you to reconsider?

3. One of the ways we need to be communicating with God is thanking Him for the wisdom He has given us in His Word that helps us to walk with Him. Take a moment and think about something from God's Word (maybe even this psalm) that has really helped you lately, from either your reading of the Bible, a sermon, or a book. Then honestly thank God for that wisdom, and explain to Him how it has helped you.

Chapter Twelve

Accessing God's Protection under Intense Fire

Psalm 56

Many don't know the name Desmond Doss. Yet many of you have probably heard of or seen the movie *Hacksaw Ridge*. Desmond Doss is the man portrayed in this historically accurate movie. Doss was a Seventh-day Adventist who didn't believe in killing. His faith in Christ was important to him, and he wanted to serve his Lord faithfully. So in a surprise to many, when World War II broke out, Doss unexpectedly enlisted in the army.

Doss didn't see himself as a conscientious objector but as a conscientious cooperator. Unlike most objectors, he was more than proud to wear the uniform, salute the American flag, and serve his country. When he enlisted, however, his views weren't understood and he was bullied and harassed. His superiors tried desperately to get him discharged from the army on the grounds of mental instability. Yet a 1940 law allowed conscientious objectors to serve the war effort in noncombatant positions.

Doss trained as a medic, reasoning that he could be like Christ: saving life instead of taking life. The film *Hacksaw Ridge* shows Doss during the battle of Okinawa. In the spring of 1945, Doss's company faced a daunting task: climb a steep, jagged cliff, called Hacksaw Ridge, up to a plateau where thousands of heavily armed Japanese soldiers waited for them. The terrain was treacherous, full of caves and holes. And the Japanese were dug in underground.

Many Americans were dying in the attack, so everyone was ordered to retreat. But Doss disobeyed orders and kept going back to get wounded men and pull them to safety. Now, the Japanese hated medics and targeted them by looking for their insignia. If they killed medics, there would be no one to care for wounded soldiers, and they would lose morale.

For hours Doss dragged men to the edge of Hacksaw Ridge and then lowered them to safety. The whole time he was praying, "Lord, please help me get one more."[1] Through that long day he was credited with saving seventy-five men, gaining the men's trust and respect. Two weeks later he was wounded by shrapnel from a grenade and shot by a Japanese sniper but refused to be rescued until another wounded soldier was taken first.

He went on to receive the Medal of Honor. On the day he was given the honor, Doss told President Truman that he owed his life to God, who he believed saved him on numerous occasions so that he might perform the duties he did in battle.[2]

Doss had learned how to access God's protection under fierce attack. His strong faith had equipped him to do what few others would attempt. A man continually charging into intense fire, unarmed, seems ridiculous. What could give a man such courage? What could he be trusting in that would allow him to face *that* kind of danger? This brings us to Psalm 56, where David also needs to access God's protection. So we begin with . . .

The Fierce Attack to Expect

We are often surprised at the intensity of attack we can face. Life is dangerous and difficult. Doss wasn't ignorant of what lay ahead of him when he went into battle on the island of Okinawa, because he had already performed valiantly on Guam doing the same kind of things. He knew how fierce the attack could be. So did David, so he writes,

> For the choir director; according to Jonath elem rehokim. A Mikhtam of David, when the Philistines seized him in Gath.
>
> Be gracious to me, O God, for man has trampled upon me; fighting all day long he oppresses me. My foes have trampled upon me all day long, for they are many who fight proudly against me. When I am afraid, I will put my trust in You. In God, whose word I praise, in God I have put my trust; I shall not be afraid. What can mere man do to me? All day long they distort my words; all their thoughts are against me for evil. They attack, they lurk, they watch my steps, as they have waited to take my life. Because of wickedness, cast them forth, in anger put down the peoples, O God! (vv. 1–7)

The words *Jonath elem rehokim* are translated by Dr. Derek Kidner as "according to the dove on far off Terebinths."[3] Some say it is the name of a tune or song. Some say it is a reference to Psalm 55:6, where David writes, "I said, Oh, that I had wings like a dove! I would fly away and be at rest." One commentator has translated these same words as "the silent dove in distant lands,"[4] while another has translated it "a dove on distant oaks."[5] The idea here would possibly be to sing the words to Psalm 56 to the same tune as Psalm 55. But this is all conjecture.

Mikhtam, some commentators believe, comes from a word that means "to cover."[6] The idea may be that what is covered is the lips, so this would be translated "a silent prayer." We find the title *Mikhtam* also in Psalm 16 and Psalms 55–60, all psalms of David and all where it appears David could not have prayed these prayers out loud given his current circumstances.

David found himself in situations where he could not go to the tabernacle—he was in trouble, on the run, a refugee. There are times when we find ourselves in situations where we don't have time to go to church, call a pastor, talk to Christian friends, read any commentaries or blogs, or listen to any YouTube videos. We are in serious trouble, and all we have time for is a silent prayer. Yet how powerful are those quick, silent prayers. Of such, this psalm is made.

David begins, "Be gracious to me, O God, for man has trampled upon me" (v. 1). He is saying, "God, I'm getting clobbered by people! They are coming after me from every direction and are slamming me!" We are given the historical context for this psalm: "When the Philistines seized him in Gath." In 1 Samuel 21:10–15 we read of David running for his life from King Saul, who thought David was a threat to his throne. David's own people were tracking him all over Israel, and eventually the only place David could retreat to safety was to leave Israel and enter Gath.

This shows the kind of situation David was in. Gath was not the place David wanted to show his face. Why? You might remember that David had once killed a giant named Goliath. Goliath was the hometown hero of the land of Gath, the town of the Philistines. But things were so bad in Israel for David, Gath was the only place to go.

When he showed up, he was immediately recognized. As we read in 1 Samuel 21:11, they had the man of whom the women had sung, "Saul has slain his thousands, and David his ten thousands."

Out of the Fire, into the Frying Pan

There was a famous picture years ago of a grizzly bear in the middle of a river with his mouth open and a large salmon jumping into the bear's mouth. Of course, that was ironic. That salmon had been born in that river and as a young fish had swum into the ocean, escaping many hungry predators to return to its native river to spawn. Yet the river had many falls, so the only way the salmon could go upstream was to make a series of jumps. This fish had the bad luck to jump right into the gaping mouth of a grizzly.

In a sense, that's what happened to David. And it looked like he was finished. But God gave David an idea. He pretended to be insane. "So he disguised his sanity before them, and acted insanely in their hands, and scribbled on the doors of the gate, and let his saliva run down into his beard" (1 Samuel 21:13). What was the response? "Then Achish said to his servants, 'Behold, you see the man behaving as a madman. Why do you bring him to me? Do I lack madmen, that you have brought this one to act the madman in my presence? Shall this one come into my house?'" (vv. 14–15).

If you will forgive the pun, there was actually some method to David's madness. "In the ancient world, insane people were regarded as harbingers of evil, and to harm them might provoke the gods."[7] God rescues us in mysterious ways at times.

David is like a sheep between two packs of wolves. "For man has trampled upon me; fighting all day long he oppresses me. My foes have trampled upon me all day long, for they are many who fight proudly against me" (vv. 1–2).

There are times when our troubles are unrelenting "all day long." We wake up with them and go to bed with them. Problems, challenges, obstacles, opposition, discouragements, and frustrations siphon the joy out of our lives. It is incessant. David continues, "When I am afraid, I will put my trust in You. In God, whose word I praise, in God I have put my trust; I shall not be afraid. What can mere man do to me?" (vv. 3–4).

David admits two seemingly contradictory truths: "I am afraid" and "I shall not be afraid." David admits he's scared. Things in life frighten us, but there is no shame in being afraid. It's what we do when that fear hits that matters. "I shall not be afraid." I shall not allow fear to rule me.

How do you talk to God about your greatest fears? We are often hesitant to admit our fears to anyone—even God. We need to learn to be honest with God and admit it when we are afraid. It is not failure to be afraid—it is human. Jesus feared the separation from his Father He would experience on the cross—and allowed us to witness it. Jesus was honest with His Father. It is not unspiritual to admit fear to God.

David decides his only hope is to put his trust in God because he can't beat his enemies. David had to continually put his trust in God because fear pops up in his life over and over—just as it does in our lives. Putting your trust in God when you are afraid isn't a one-off—I did it once and don't need to do it again. The fear we subdue once will rise again within us.

New or immature Christians can get discouraged when they have faced a fear with trust in God and seen victory, only to have that same fear later reappear. Wait, they think. I thought I had faith and that banished my fear. But it's back, so did I really have faith? Yes, you did! You chose in that moment to focus on God and His power, and it diminished the fear. But we don't always remain focused on God, do we? And there are many voices speaking in our ear, not just God. Each time we are afraid, we have to consciously decide who we are going to listen to, what we are going to truly trust.

In George MacDonald's fairy tale *The Princess and the Goblin*, the young princess is being chased by a strange goblin creature—at least she thought she was. So she ran wildly, even when her running actually took her into danger. As

MacDonald wrote, "Not daring to look behind her, she rushed straight out of the gate and up the mountain. It was foolish indeed—thus to run farther and farther from all who could help her, as if she had been seeking a fit spot for the goblin creature to eat her at his leisure; *but that is the way fear serves us: it always sides with the thing we're afraid of*" (emphasis added).[8] The goblin wasn't chasing her after all, but her fear had sided with the goblin and caused her to run in terror.

I have noticed that my faith in God is strongest when nothing is at stake—when I have enough money, my health is good, and all is peaceful at work and at home and in my world. In those moments I am an imposing tower of faith and trust. I can trust God for anything in those moments. But when I'm really worried about something bad that might happen to me, I learn what my faith is really made of.

When I don't have enough money, when a test comes back saying I have cancer, when I may lose my job, when I may lose a precious relationship, when I may lose my reputation . . . in those moments I learn what my faith is really made of. To trust God doesn't mean I don't feel fear—it means I don't let that fear control me. I don't let it knock me off my faith. David says, "In God, whose word I praise, in God I have put my trust; I shall not be afraid" (v. 4).

The writer of Hebrews quotes these words in 13:5–6: "For He Himself has said, 'I will never desert you, nor will I ever forsake you.' So that we confidently say, 'The LORD is my helper, I will not be afraid, what will man do to me?'" Yes, the Sauls and the Philistines of the world are against me, but if God is for me, the odds are always in my favor. Who can box with God? David continues, "All day long they distort my words; all their thoughts are against me for evil. They attack, they lurk, they watch my steps, as they have waited to take my life" (vv. 5–6).

When I read this, I couldn't help but think, Just another day on Twitter. This is life on social media these days for the righteous. Cancel culture is not some new creation of man—it's been around for a long time. It's what put Jesus on the cross.

Jesus's enemies thought, If we can just silence Him forever, He'll have no more influence, and we can regain ours! But since God was for Jesus, the resurrection ensured Jesus's influence would prevail forever and His enemies would be silenced forever.

Then David writes, "Because of wickedness, cast them forth, in anger put down the peoples, O God!" (v. 7). David is a warrior and a great leader, but he knows when he's in over his head. God needs to help him—that's his only hope. But then David brings up . . .

The Promise to Claim

What is it that we cling to when the attack is fierce and unrelenting? It is the promise that God is on our side and will ultimately make sure we prevail. So David writes,

> You have taken account of my wanderings; put my tears in Your bottle. Are they not in Your book? Then my enemies will turn back in the day when I call; this I know, that God is for me. In God, whose word I praise, in the LORD, whose word I praise, in God I have put my trust, I shall not be afraid. What can man do to me? (vv. 8–11)

David knows he is not telling God anything He doesn't already know. God knows how David has had to run from Saul and from Achish. God knows of his desperate wanderings. But God also knows of David's tears—his very real tears of fear and desperation. He says that God has put his tears in a bottle. It is an incredibly tender and touching picture of God's love for us.

Think about this: the creator of all, the greatest power and mind in existence, the very reason for existence . . . cares how you feel and what you are going through, and He has a record of all your tears.

Over the years traditions have sprung up of people collecting tears in bottles. It is said the practice began in 400 BC—when women's husbands went off to war, the women kept the tears they shed in bottles. They were called lachrymatory bottles. If her loved one died, she put the bottle in his grave as a sign of love and respect.

During the Civil War, some men left their wives a tear bottle, hoping that upon their return the bottles would be full—signifying their wives' sorrow at their danger. Sadly, many men never returned. The bottle became a token of remembrance. Often when a loved one died, the mourner would go to the grave a year later to pour out the bottle on the grave, signifying her period of mourning was over.

We need to be reminded that God cares for us, that He is supporting *us* and not our enemy. "Then my enemies will turn back in the day when I call; this I know, that God is for me" (v. 9). What promise does David claim during his terrible fear? "God is for me!" Where have we heard that before? In Romans! Paul asks, "What then shall we say to these things? If God is for us, who is against us?" (8:31).

We have the promise of God that as His children, He is for us. That promise is so important to David. "In God, whose word I praise, in the LORD, whose word I praise" (v. 10), he repeats himself. It's not just wishful thinking—it's the promise of God. He is for us! Do you know this?

During World War II, the US Army deployed what became known as the "Ghost Army." It was comprised of artists, set designers, actors, and sound-stage technicians whose main job was to deceive the Germans and draw fire and attention away from where the real fighting was. So they created inflatable tanks and recorded sound effects to mimic whole battalions where there wasn't a single soldier. It was wildly successful, credited with saving thousands of lives through deception.[9]

Satan often deploys his own ghost armies to threaten and deceive us into believing we are lost and forsaken. He magnifies imaginary dangers to convince us we have no hope. Our only hope is to cling to that which we know to be true—the Word of God and His promises.

Before David will repeat "What can mere man do to me?" he has already affirmed that "God is for me"! David has learned that truth through experience. God had allowed him to face down lethal dangers as a shepherd from both bear and lion and come out alive. When he faced Goliath, he already had experience with the truth that "God is for me." He didn't beat the bear and lion because he was such a great fighter but because God had helped him.

David had learned and internalized that lesson. Have you? Life is always going to throw problems at you—you have an enemy. Unless you realize that God is truly for you because you are His child, every time you face trouble you will go into anxiety and stress mode. Your joy and peace will be transient. Yes, things are difficult. Yes, things aren't better yet. Yes, you can't see the end of the tunnel yet—but God will guide you and keep you through this.

Every time we are afraid, we need to stop focusing on our fear and refocus on our promise from God. These promises need to be claimed, not merely admired as spiritual trinkets.

We are a people who take advantage of promises made us by friends, companies, and government. When we feel they aren't being honored, we recite them to the responsible party. Do you have the courage to recite God's promises to Him in your prayers? He is not in the least offended by it since they are *His* promises—and He truly intends to keep them, even if it looks like He won't.

Begin to incorporate into your prayers His promises to you and your hope and faith in those promises. And even the weakness of your faith at that moment—He knows that too.

Finally, assessing God's protection involves . . .

The Vow to Keep

When God keeps His promises to us, we should keep our promises to Him. David had obviously made a vow to God of what he would do if God would rescue him. So we read,

> Your vows are binding upon me, O God; I will render thank offerings to You. For You have delivered my soul from death, indeed my feet from stumbling, so that I may walk before God in the light of the living. (vv. 12–13)

Here is the point of the psalm. God answered David's prayer and did deliver him out of danger from both Saul and Achish. David now does what so few believers do—he remembers to thank God for it.

In Michael Medved's book *The American Miracle: Divine Providence in the Rise of the Republic*, he tells of a meeting Abraham Lincoln had with one of his colonels after the battle of Gettysburg. Lincoln had visited general Daniel Edgar Sickles, who had been wounded, and Colonel Rusling wrote down their conversation. General Sickles asked Lincoln if he had shared the fear everyone seemed to have that the Confederates would win at Gettysburg. Lincoln responded,

> In the pinch of your campaign up there, when everybody seemed panic stricken, and nobody could tell what was going to happen, oppressed by the gravity of our affairs, I went into my room one day and locked the door and got down on my knees before Almighty God and prayed to him mightily for victory at Gettysburg. I told him that this was his war, and our cause his cause, but that we couldn't stand another Fredericksburg or Chancellorsville. And I then and there made a solemn vow to Almighty God that if he would stand by our boys at Gettysburg, I would stand by him. And he did, and I will. And after that, I don't know how it was and I can't explain it, but

soon a sweet comfort crept into my soul that things would go alright at Gettysburg, and this is why I had no fears about you.[10]

It is tempting to romanticize David, to think him a person we could never be like. But he wasn't that unlike us. The same God who rescued David and who rescued the Union, rescues us. It is no greater task to God to save someone from a lion, or a bear, or a jealous king, or a Confederate army with tons of positive momentum, than to save from emotional stress and fear, relational conflict, political pressures, financial stresses, overwhelming grief or sadness, or physical pain and suffering. And remember, many of the things we fear are no more than Satan's ghost armies. They aren't real dangers and won't really hurt us. We just fear they will.

> Many of the things we fear are no more than Satan's ghost armies. They aren't real dangers and won't really hurt us.

But when we ask God to deliver us, and He does, we are under obligation to glorify and thank Him for it. This is where too often we fail, and it is to the detriment of our faith. When we remember how God has helped us, it strengthens us for the next time we need faith. When we forget how He's helped us, it weakens us for the next time we need faith.

What does David say? "For You have delivered my soul from death, indeed my feet from stumbling, so that I may walk before God in the light of the living" (v. 13). David trusted God's promise, and God did not disappoint him. Why does David say twice, "In God, whose word I praise, in God whose word I praise" (vv. 4, 10)? It was God's promise that had brought him confidence that God would ultimately rescue him. That's why he can say twice, "What can man do to me?" (vv. 4, 11).

Where Is Jesus in Psalm 56?

In verses 1–7 we can see Jesus harassed by the Pharisees and scribes as they constantly sought to trap Him in some way. In verses 8–11 we see the attitude of

Jesus on the cross: "What can man do to me?" As in, "He can take away my life but cannot touch my soul. The Father will yet raise me to life." Finally in verses 12–13 we see Jesus's joy in the resurrection. "Your vows are binding upon me, O God; I will render thank offerings to You. For You have delivered my soul from death, indeed my feet from stumbling, so that I may walk before God in the light of the living."

The promise of God is our confidence—if we allow it to be. We can expect fierce attacks at times, but when we do, we have promises of God to claim. And when we claim them and stand on them, we must be prepared to keep our vow to thank and praise God when He delivers us. It honors God and strengthens our faith.

Recall how for hours, under intense fire, Desmond Doss dragged men to the edge of Hacksaw Ridge and then lowered them to safety. The whole time he was praying, "Lord, please help me get one more." What Doss did in a small way, Jesus did in an infinitely greater way. He endured the fiercest attack ever launched in order to drag us to safety, always seeking "one more." That's the gospel. And maybe you're the one more Jesus wants to drag to safety today. Maybe you're finally ready to say, "Jesus, I'm ready—take me!"

QUESTIONS

1. There are times when we, like David, are in a bad place. We wake up with our problems, they are with us all day long, and we go to bed with them. These problems are so large and intense that, like David, we struggle with trust. What are you struggling to trust God with today?

2. When we experience such fears, we forget that the voice of God and the words of Scripture are not the only voices speaking to us. What are some of the other voices speaking to us and inciting us to stop trusting God and fear again?

3. Satan employs ghost armies, magnifying imaginary dangers within us until we are petrified with fear. What are some imaginary dangers you have feared in your past that never came to pass? How many times have you worried about something that never happened?

Chapter Thirteen

You Are the Object of His Attention

Psalm 139

We recently watched *Captain America: The Winter Soldier*. It's one of the Marvel Comics movies. It has a fascinating plot point: in a desire to protect our country from hostile acts, S.H.I.E.L.D. (Strategic Homeland Intervention, Enforcement and Logistics Division) created the latest top-secret project called "Operation Insight," which will launch three aircraft carriers into space, linked by a satellite to protect the world.

What S.H.I.E.L.D. officials don't realize is that S.H.I.E.L.D. has been infiltrated at the highest levels by people who believe the best way to deter crime is to kill criminals even before they act. They have developed complicated computer algorithms that can predict crime and the criminal. Any person who might pose any danger, or might be seen as trying to stop them from fulfilling their mission, is targeted. Captain America has to try to stop this before it happens.

What is fascinating in the world today is the amount of data computers are able to collect from people because of the use of electronics, which can be traced. The amount of data that can be collected by complete strangers is staggering. People having that amount of knowledge about us scares us. What will they do with it? Can they be trusted with it? Will they use it against us? We are right to be nervous.

Many of us had no idea we were the object of so much attention by complete strangers. But in Psalm 139, we are going to learn that we are far, far more the object of God's attention, and that far from frightening us, it should give us great comfort and encouragement. We will be literally *stunned* by the intimate attention God gives and has given each and every one of us. Being the object of His attention means . . .

God Knows You Intimately

It's interesting to me how we all have a bit of (or a lot of) fear of people getting to know us too well. It's a common feeling, but why? Why are we afraid of people having that kind of knowledge of us? We do seek to hide from prying eyes. Yet David is going to remind us that there are eyes we can never hide from. So David writes,

For the choir director. A Psalm of David.

O Lord, You have searched me and known me. You know when I sit down and when I rise up; You understand my thought from afar. You scrutinize my path and my lying down, and are intimately acquainted with all my ways. Even before there is a word on my tongue, behold, O Lord, You know it all. You have enclosed me behind and before, and laid Your hand upon me. Such knowledge is too wonderful for me; it is too high, I cannot attain to it. (vv. 1–6)

We are told by many that we are merely insignificant specks in the great cosmos. The more we have learned about how large the universe really is, the more insignificant we feel. We are less than specks in eternity. Yet the Spirit of the Creator tells us a vastly different story.

We learn here that God is far greater than we ever thought and yet far more intimately concerned with us than we could have ever hoped. Here, the greatness of God leads not to feelings of insignificance but to an amazement with His intimate knowledge of our every thought and movement. We are surprised to learn that each one of us has God's undivided attention perpetually.

It is amazing how intimately involved God is with our lives. He searches us and knows us. He knows when we sit down and when we rise up. He understands what we're thinking. And it doesn't just say He *knows* what we're thinking but that He *understands* what we're thinking.

There are times when my thoughts and feelings are a jumble. I can't figure out what I really think or feel about something. But God understands where my jumbled thoughts come from and what they are connected to. When I'm in a fog, He sees through that fog instantly. It's why God knows us better than we know ourselves. He is intimately acquainted with all our ways. God does not collect trivia—He is simply aware of all that we do, think, and feel and knows why we end up thinking and feeling what we do.

And it's why David says, "Even before there is a word on my tongue, behold, O Lord, You know it all" (v. 4). We don't have to articulate our thoughts to God as we do to each other. God never has to ask, "What do you mean?" God knows what is in our hearts and minds. As Hebrews 4:13 reminds us, "There is no creature hidden from His sight, but all things are open and laid bare to the eyes of Him with whom we have to do."

The word *scrutinize* translates the Hebrew word meaning "to sift." God carefully and thoroughly sifts our choices and decisions. It's why He knows us better than we know ourselves.

God is constantly watching and understanding all we do, every second of every day. Some have labeled this psalm the "Hound of Heaven." It's from a poem, and it's widely quoted by C. S. Lewis. But what is so mind-boggling and comforting at the same time to the believer is the understanding that God is not just some great, unfeeling supercomputer collecting data to use against us.

Love-Tracking

In a Star Trek movie, a satellite from years ago went off course and had an accident and began collecting data to try to find its way home. In the process, it destroyed everything in its path. It gained the ability to use knowledge against anything in its way. When the crew from Star Trek finally landed on its surface, they realized that V'ger, as it was named, was actually the name Voyager. It was an ancient Earth probe seeking information that had gone rogue. They actually had to protect themselves from V'ger getting any more information about them, as it was used against them.

God isn't like that. His interest in us is personal, intimate, and burning with compassion. He doesn't view us the way the internet does or the government does or companies do. He knows us intimately and personally. He is love-tracking us. All His intentions toward us are good. His goal is our rescue and salvation.

But some people *want* to hide from God. They want to hide their thoughts, actions, plans, and ambitions. It's a major reason some want to divest themselves of the idea of God completely. They don't want to be known that well or intimately. They resent the intrusion. They want to deactivate their God account.

But you can't. You can't hide from God any more than you can hide yourself by running naked through a crowded grocery store. Actually, this knowledge should be a comfort, but we often feel like we have to hide from God. David continues, "Behold, O Lord, You know it all. You have enclosed me behind and before, and laid Your hand upon me. Such knowledge is too wonderful for me; it is too high, I cannot attain to it" (vv. 4–6).

The word *enclosed* comes from a Hebrew word for the besieging of a city in battle and closing off all escape routes. It means "to be hemmed in." This strikes a note with me. There have been many times when I have felt hemmed in by God. I wanted to escape a particular situation desperately and couldn't.

God, in His great wisdom, knowing how we really need to grow, keeps us from escaping the very experiences that will help us do precisely that. Thinking we will find peace and contentment by escaping, God closes the doors because He knows peace and contentment won't be found that way by us.

So there is a job you want to escape, a relationship you want to escape, a danger you want to escape, an experience you want to escape, a sickness you want to escape, a loss you want to escape. But God encloses you . . . so you have to deal with issues you would rather avoid. You have to lean in to God, to trust Him in ways you'd rather not. I have been hemmed in by God numerous times, and every time it was for my good. Each time I came out more like Jesus than I had been and more at peace than I had been.

God encloses you . . . so you have to deal with issues you would rather avoid.

Shutting off our escape routes is an act of love. He is guiding us wisely and lovingly where we need to be so we can be the kind of people who can embrace peace and contentment and joy. Annie Johnson Flint wrote a poem expressing this very experience of feeling "pressed":

Pressed
Pressed out of measure and pressed to all length.
Pressed so intensely it seems beyond strength;
Pressed in the body, pressed in the soul,
Pressed in the mind till the dark surges roll;
Pressure by foes and pressure by friends;
Pressure on pressure, till life nearly ends;
Pressed into loving the staff and the rod,
Pressed into knowing no helper but God
Pressed into liberty where nothing clings;
Pressed into faith for impossible things;
Pressed into loving a life in the Lord,
Pressed into living a Christ-life outpoured. [1]

She understood God's enclosing was an act of deep, deep love. David simply says of all these truths: "Such knowledge is too wonderful for me; it is too high, I cannot attain to it" (v. 6).

Are there times when the wonder of God, His power, His omniscience, His omnipresence cause you to be in awe? Have you ever confessed your awe to Him? Certainly God wants to hear and answer your prayers, but you were designed and created to give Him glory.

As weak, as inadequate, as feeble as it may be, God welcomes our praise and awe to Him in prayer. Praise should flow from our lips and hearts as easily as prayers. What a blessing it is to sit or walk and share with God how wonderful and marvelous He is. These, too, are honest feelings.

Being the object of God's attention means God knows you intimately, but it also means . . .

God Is Extremely Attentive to You

As anyone who has sat in a busy restaurant with too few waiters and waitresses can attest, someone can know you are there and that you want attention, and still manage to conspicuously avoid you. But David knows that God doesn't just know you intimately but is intensely attentive to you. So David writes,

Where can I go from Your Spirit? Or where can I flee from Your presence? If I ascend to heaven, You are there; if I make my bed in Sheol, behold, You are there. If I take the wings of the dawn, if I dwell in the remotest part of the sea, even there Your hand will lead me, and Your right hand will lay hold of me. If I say, "Surely the darkness will overwhelm me, and the light around me will be night," even the darkness is not dark to You, and the night is as bright as the day. Darkness and light are alike to You. (vv. 7–12)

God never loses track of us. There is no place in the great cosmos that is hidden from His eyes. From Sheol (the place of the departed dead) to heaven, He sees it all. From the most remote place on Earth to the deepest part of the sea, God tracks us.

There are people vying to be the first colonizers on Mars. They are willing to try to fly to Mars, and live in a colony, and never see Earth or their loved ones here again. It's not just spaceman hype—it's a real venture. I have no doubt that at some point in the future, if Christ does not come first, that they will make it. When that happens, He will be there and be with them all the way there.

"Where can I go from Your Spirit? Or where can I flee from Your presence?" (v. 7). Here, David has a moment of consideration. Sometimes we can feel trapped by God, or as he has said, "hemmed in." That urge to hide from God is as old as the garden of Eden. Adam and Eve had never felt the need to hide from God until they sinned—then they instinctively felt the need to hide from holiness. His omnipresence was no longer a comfort to them—it was a threat. Sin makes us want to hide from God.

Studies have been done showing that when young people are active in church and then go to college and get involved with sexual immorality, their attendance at church fades away. The answer is simple enough. Church reminds them of their sin, and they want to hide from God. But we can't. Like David asks, "Where could we go?" There is no hiding from God. There never was.

The word in the New Testament for Sheol is Hades—the place that Luke tells us, in Acts, could not hold our Lord. "But God raised Him up again, putting an end to the agony of death, since it was impossible for Him to be held in its power. . . . [David] looked ahead and spoke of the resurrection of the Christ, that He was neither abandoned to Hades, nor did His flesh suffer decay" (Acts 2:24, 31).

The Guardian of the Galaxy

David continues, "If I take the wings of the dawn, if I dwell in the remotest part of the sea, even there Your hand will lead me, and Your right hand will lay hold of me" (vv. 9–10). Some scholars believe this is referring to the scene at dawn, where the view stretches from the east across the sky to the west (as far as the Mediterranean Sea). The wings of the dawn is the speed of light. If David could take the speed of light and hide in the remotest part of the sea, or the distance beyond even sight, "even there Your hand will lead me, and Your right hand will lay hold of me."

But distance isn't the only way to hide from God. So David says, "If I say, 'Surely the darkness will overwhelm me, and the light around me will be night,' even the darkness is not dark to You, and the night is as bright as the day. Darkness and light are alike to You" (vv. 11–12).

Even the complete absence of light, in which men could not travel, cannot hide us from God. This is David's way of articulating the doctrine of God's omnipresence. He is everywhere present at once. He's not 70 percent present in some places and 30 percent present in others. Every single place God is, He is completely present and aware of all. And being everywhere present at once, He is all-powerful and all-knowing at every moment and in every place.

If, as some posit, our world is filled with millions of advanced and powerful alien civilizations scattered throughout the galaxies and across the cosmos, and they all rebelled against God at once (a future Marvel's Avengers movie, I'm sure), God would be able to bring all His power to bear in every place at once without ever depleting His strength. He is, to coin a Marvel title, the ultimate Guardian of the Galaxy.

It's not that you simply can't avoid Him but that He is intensely focused upon you. Let's not miss what David is doing. David is sharing with God what He has learned about God, truths that now help him navigate his life more effectively. There is a place in our prayers to God to share what we have learned from Him.

We remember ways we tried to hide from God, or times we wanted to. What David does so beautifully in the Psalms is *talk* with God. Conversation. Too frequently our time with God consists of filling out mental applications for help, while disregarding the Person we are speaking to.

I love complimenting people who I see do wonderful things. It brings me joy to see them so appreciative. So often people are not praised for what they do or who they are. Our God is not a force—He is a person! While He does not need our praise, it blesses Him. Furthermore . . .

God Thinks You Are Incredibly Important

Being known by God isn't the same as being important to God. We know many things that we don't feel are all that important. Yet David understands how important God sees him, so he writes,

> For You formed my inward parts; You wove me in my mother's womb.
> I will give thanks to You, for I am fearfully and wonderfully made;
> wonderful are Your works, and my soul knows it very well. My frame
> was not hidden from You, when I was made in secret, and skillfully
> wrought in the depths of the earth; Your eyes have seen my unformed
> substance; and in Your book were all written the days that were
> ordained for me, when as yet there was not one of them. (vv. 13–16)

Again, God's omnipresence is mentioned. God even knows about us in the womb. Years ago when I was still in seminary, my pastor shared a discussion he'd had with a neighbor about God. He told him about God's omnipresence, that God was everywhere at once. The neighbor smirked and then pointed sarcastically to a pile of dog poop on the lawn in front of them. "So you're telling me that God is in there?" My pastor paused for a moment and then replied, "Let me put it this way—if you could find a way to get into that pile of dog poop, you could not escape from God."

"For You formed my inward parts; You wove me in my mother's womb" (v. 13). The *You* here in the Hebrew is emphatic. "*You*, God, not anyone or anything else, formed me and wove me in my mother's womb." The Hebrew verb *sanak*, translated "wove me," is the word used for knitting things together, like cloth or a thicket.

God didn't just set up the reproductive system and let it run its course. He micromanages it. You *formed* me. You *wove* me. He knits all our organs, blood, veins, arteries, muscles, tendons, and bones together to form us. Charles Swindoll paraphrases it this way: "My skeleton and bones were not hidden from You when I was made in that concealed place of protection (womb), when my veins and arteries were skillfully embroidered together in variegated colors like fine needle point."[2]

"I will give thanks to You, for I am fearfully and wonderfully made; wonderful are Your works, and my soul knows it very well" (v. 14). David is saying, "All these mysteries, I thank you for." David wasn't just thankful there was a great God but that God allowed David to experience His greatness by the way he had been created. "My frame was not hidden from You, When I was made in secret, and skillfully wrought in the depths of the earth; Your eyes have seen my unformed substance; and in Your book were all written the days that were ordained for me, when as yet there was not one of them" (vv. 15–16).

God oversaw David's development in the womb (depths of the earth), and the "unformed substance" was David's fetus. The word for *unformed substance* means to "fold together, wrap up." It is referring to an embryo. God watched over David in the womb when he was but an embryo. A person does not have to be born to be known by God! Life begins in the womb and God Himself is the author of life. We are not ultimately its maker. God is.

God knows how many days you will live, how many beats your heart will have, how many breaths you will take, how many steps you will take—before you are even born. And it causes David to say,

How precious also are Your thoughts to me, O God! How vast is the sum of them! If I should count them, they would outnumber the sand. When I awake, I am still with You. (vv. 17–18)

Do you hear David's wonder and gratitude in these words? As he thinks about the greatness of God, he realizes how that greatness has been directed in deep love to him. He finds all those thoughts "precious."

How pleasant it is when Annette and I are separated and I get a text from her asking how my day is going. I am reminded that I am on her mind a lot. When was the last time you thanked God for His intimate involvement in your life?

I love Annette and think about her often. Yet those thoughts, as frequent as they are, could be counted. There are currently around eight billion people in the world. God is giving each one of them His undivided attention—because He can. And He knows all who were born before that, because they are still alive to Him. And He's doing all that simultaneously. He is literally undistractable.

We often talk about multitasking, but we aren't really doing that. We are simply able to change our focus from one thing to another with amazing speed. But we are only focusing a percentage of our attention on one thing, and when we do that, we are simultaneously diminishing the amount we focus on something else.[3] But God is the ultimate divine multitasker, and it is not even a stretch for Him. He never stops thinking about anyone! Let that sink in.

But, last of all, and as a result of all of this . . .

God Expects Us to Trust Him

God doesn't tell us things about Himself so we are more informed but so that our hearts and minds will be transformed. All of this should lead to something, so David writes,

> O that You would slay the wicked, O God; depart from me, therefore, men of bloodshed. For they speak against You wickedly, and Your enemies take Your name in vain. Do I not hate those who hate You, O Lord? And do I not loathe those who rise up against You? I hate them with the utmost hatred; they have become my enemies. Search me, O God, and know my heart; try me and know my anxious thoughts; and see if there be any hurtful way in me, and lead me in the everlasting way. (vv. 19–24)

In light of all that David has said about the greatness of God, watching the evil take His name in vain and mock Him just fries David. He has a holy indignation. People who have no concept of the goodness and greatness of God belittle and ridicule Him. David asks God to get rid of them. Derek Kidner wrote about David's plea, "For all its vehemence, the hatred in this passage is not spite, but zeal for God."[4]

When you love someone intensely, you get livid when someone belittles them. Many people who would criticize this in God, don't criticize it in themselves. When someone they love or admire is criticized, they are incensed, angry, and even prone to violence, as we see so much today. Yet David does not plan to become violent. He simply asks God to deal with them appropriately.

Many believe that zeal for God leads to hate. No, it leads to a hatred of evil and the evil that people do and say. And here we come to the question . . .

Where Is Jesus in Psalm 139?

In John 22:16–17 Jesus drove the money changers out of the temple. "And to those who were selling the doves He said, 'Take these things away; stop making My Father's house a place of business.' His disciples remembered that it was written, 'Zeal for Your house will consume Me.'"

Jesus hated the activity of the money changers and drove them out, but later He would die upon the cross for those same people. You can hate the sin and still love the sinner. As the apostle Paul reminds us, "God demonstrates His own love toward us, in that while we were yet sinners, Christ died for us" (Romans 5:8). God hated the sin and punished it on the cross, but He also died for us on that cross because He loved us. A true zeal for the real God will lead to hating sin but loving the sinner; Christ fulfilled this truth. And in John 1 we learn that Jesus created all, so we see here the Creator describing His creation. Jesus wove us all together (John 1:3).

While it's easy to see the sin and frailty in others, it can be hard to see it in ourselves. So here David invites God to "search me, O God, and know my heart; try me and know my anxious thoughts; and see if there be any hurtful way in me" (vv. 23–24). David welcomes God's gaze upon him because there may be sinful thoughts, ambitions, or dreams that would destroy David if he was allowed to indulge them. David wants these purged from his soul. He doesn't want to be hurtful to man or God.

First responders like police, firefighters, and paramedics respond to emergencies, only to find at times that the person in danger won't let them in or won't cooperate. People can be suspicious, stubborn, ignorant, and cantankerous. But despite all this, the first responders force the issue. If the door isn't opened, they force it in. They will help those who don't even want to be helped, if necessary.

It's the same with God. If there is a poisonous idea, attitude, opinion, He will force the issue. But from experience I have found that He is gentle and persuasive when I give Him permission to search me and evict whatever needs to be evicted in my heart. And I have seen God change feelings I gave Him permission to change if I was in the wrong.

How did the psalm open? "You have searched me." The first is a bow to the inevitable. The second is an invitation, a desire of David's. "Search me, O God."

But what David ultimately wants is for God to "lead me in the everlasting way." All that David has learned about God has not caused him to distrust God but to trust Him all the more. God's knowledge of us, His attention, is for our good.

God *has* searched you. He knows all about you. *All* about you. And yet, His love for you is of an intensity to take our breath away. He also knew His Son, searching His heart as well. Then He pronounced, "This is my beloved Son in whom I am well pleased" (Matthew 3:17). After divine examination, no sin was found in Jesus. God the Father sent His Son Jesus to lead us in the everlasting way.

And we see Jesus in verse 16. "And in Your book were all written the days that were ordained for me, when as yet there was not one of them." The prophesies written hundreds of years before Jesus's birth revealed the coming Son. He who was perfect in every way, knowing all our imperfections ahead of time, came and rescued us anyway.

Jesus perfectly emulates the Father's love, for it is His love too. Now, all that is left is to respond back to Him with trust, for who else knows you as much as Jesus, and still loves you this much? Take a few moments and just be honest with God in prayer. But this time, approach Him with confidence.

It's time we started being . . . honest with God!

QUESTIONS

1. David says, "You have enclosed me behind and before." There are times when we also feel hemmed in by God. We desperately want to escape a situation, and we can't. Are you in such a situation now? What would you desperately like to escape but can't?

2. Annie Johnson Flint's poem speaks to the knowledge that God hemming us in is an act of deep, deep love. She describes all the ways she felt pressed. List some ways you feel pressed right now. What do you think God might be trying to do in your life through this pressing?

3. When was the last time you prayed David's prayer, inviting God to search your heart and see if there is any hurtful way in you? After thinking and praying about it, write down what you feel God might be leading you to remove from your life that is hurtful.

Discussion and Reflection Questions

Chapter One
Honest to God

1. Read Luke 24:44. What did Jesus say about the Psalms in this passage? How might we read the Psalms differently when we consider this truth?

2. We can, at times, be afraid to share with others (even Christians or God Himself) what we are truly feeling about our circumstances. Have there been times in your life when you have been hesitant to share with God (or others) what you are truly feeling? If so, why?

3. There are times when the things we believe about God and how we feel about God at the moment are not the same. The Psalms reveal true believers sharing both doubts and fears with God. Do you feel safe sharing both these things with God? If so, why? If not, why not?

For Further Study

Spend some time thinking and meditating on all Jesus meant about Himself being revealed in the Psalms in Luke 24:44. Commit to read the psalm the next chapter refers to, and practice this before reading every new chapter in this book.

Action Item

This might be a good time to practice being honest with God. Perhaps there is an issue on your heart or mind that you have not shared with God, fearing it would reveal a lack of faith or the presence of doubt. Knowing now that God not only invites that honesty but has revealed it in the Scriptures through the Psalms, take some quiet time with God and just be honest with Him. He has been waiting for this. It's time to start the honesty!

Chapter Two
Setting Up a Living Trust (Psalm 4)

1. We all know how important trust is in our relationships with others. We also know how hard it can be. Why do you think trust is so hard in our relationship with God?

2. We are prone to "meditate" upon our problem and not upon God. Perhaps a good exercise would be to stop worrying about your problem and begin remembering how faithful God has always been to you and dwelling upon His character, displayed so vividly on the cross. How do you think that doing that in the issue you are facing now might help?

3. Is there a sin still attached to you that is slowly draining your joy and weakening your relationship with your Lord? Ask yourself whether this sin is more precious and fulfilling to you than the Lord. Are you trusting that sin or pleasure to be what only God can be for you?

4. What does our society tell us will show us good? What things does it promote that promise to deliver joy and happiness? How many can you think of?

5. What is something that threatens you right now? You don't feel safe because of that presence in your life. Is the danger real or imagined?

For Further Study

We saw Jesus in Psalm 4. As you look at Psalm 4, where can you see hints of Jesus's life and ministry that were not covered in this chapter?

Action Item

Share honestly with God anything evil or unkind people have been saying or doing toward you. Remind the Lord of what He has already done in your life, as you would for a good friend who had shown you a great kindness. What is it you truly want to say to God?

Chapter Three

Sin and Its Discontents (Psalm 6)

1. Is there a broken or fractured relationship in your life right now? How has it affected your relationship with this person or persons? How is it affecting your life and joy? Why are these so painful? Why can't we just get over it?

2. Have you ever experienced God's discipline, a time when you have walked away from Him in some way and He has brought distress to draw you back? What was that period like?

3. There are times when we are so sad, so distressed, so hopeless that our prayers are little more than gasps. We seem to have no more words. When you experience these times, what are the few words you use to call out to Him? What do you think you are truly asking God to do in those moments?

4. When you've struggled with an unconfessed, unabandoned sin, how did God create within you a deep desire to return to fellowship with Him? What did you miss most and want back?

5. Crying is a relief outlet God has created for us to release tension and gain relief when we are sad or brokenhearted. Do you struggle with crying (either in public or private)? Why or why not?

6. Sometimes when we are going through suffering, our Lord brings us nevertheless a period of calm and unexpected strength in the midst of our storm. Have you ever experienced this? Did it surprise you?

For Further Study

Where do *you* see Jesus in Psalm 6?

Action Item

If you are going through a time of suffering that you feel *may* be connected to a sin that you have not completely abandoned, find a quiet time and place and pray this prayer of David back to God, becoming the "I" of the psalm. Let David's words be yours.

Chapter Four

The Question Everyone Wants to Ask God (Psalm 10)

1. Have you ever trusted God to keep you safe from something and He didn't? How did it affect your prayers? What part of God's character did you begin to doubt?

2. Author Tim Keller frequently reminds us that if we leave God when He doesn't do what we expect Him to do, we're really only trusting Him to meet our own agenda. How might this have been true in your own experience? What was the agenda you expected God to meet?

3. Read Matthew 27:45–46. Knowing that our Lord Himself prayed an honest prayer of abandonment, how does this encourage your own prayers to God? Is it wrong to share that we feel abandoned by God, even if we know that He could never truly abandon us?

4. Was Jesus disconnecting from God with this prayer? Why do you think Jesus prayed the words of Psalm 22:1 on the cross, and what does that tell us about our Lord and how He faced feelings of abandonment? To what did Jesus always return?

5. Read verses 4 and 11. What seems to give the wicked confidence in their evil activities? Can you give an example of how this happens today in your world?

6. We don't always get the *why* questions answered from God about what He allows in our lives. Where does the psalmist end up in verses 14–18, even though he never gets his questions answered? What is a *why* question you have that you have never gotten an answer to?

For Further Study

How and where do *you* see Jesus in Psalm 10? How does Isaiah 53:3–8 help you see Jesus more clearly? How do we see that Jesus's life, death, and resurrection ensured that God did not forget the afflicted?

Action Item

It's very possible, even probable, that you have been unfairly victimized in some way. And those responsible have seemingly gotten away with it. Our Lord experienced that same thing, only on a cosmic and infinite scale. Can you, for the sake of Christ and emulating Him, let go of that pain and disappointment, knowing that He will bring justice and the wicked who hurt you will not get away with it ultimately? Can you pray that kind of honest prayer to God?

Chapter Five

Joy Comes in the Morning (Psalm 30)

1.   When God answers a heartfelt prayer request of yours, who do you tell? Do you tend to keep those things to yourself or tell others about them? Why or why not?

2.   Can you think of a time when God rescued you from your own failures? How could even your failures cause you to praise Him?

3.   Take a moment and write down some important things you have received from God, whether they be physical possessions, relationships, or even abilities. Make a list. How has God uniquely blessed you? Take a moment and thank Him for these gifts.

4.   You weren't primarily created to be of value to others—you were created to glorify God. How does that help you understand your purpose in God's world and what He might bring into, or remove from, your life?

5.   Try to remember a time when God turned your sadness into joy. What did He do?

For Further Study

Where else might you see Jesus reflected in Psalm 30?

Action Item

(Choose one or try them both.)

1.   Enlist someone (or a group) in your life to share your praises and prayer requests with. Share with them what God is doing in your life, what you praise Him for, and what you are seeking Him for.

2.   Write out an Ebenezer, an example of how God has rescued you in your past and how it reflects His goodness and grace.

Chapter Six
Seeking Vindication (Psalm 35)

1. Have you asked God to come and rescue you from an evil? Have you dared ask Him to go to war with you against this evil, or have you just sought to handle it on a purely human basis? Why is it sometimes hard to ask God to do this?

2. Have you ever considered that it's OK to ask God to bring you a sense of safety and protection in the midst of your danger? Perhaps take a moment and write out just such a request to God, keeping it where you can see it regularly. God doesn't want to rescue us just from danger but also from the feeling of danger.

3. God demonstrates through this psalm, and even Jesus's life, that it's OK to ask God to bring about justice from unfair treatment. Is there something in your life right now that you need to ask God to intervene in, to bring you justice? Consider writing out just such a request to God. Be honest!

4. Have you ever been the victim of friendly fire, in which a Christian brother or sister has attacked you unjustly? How did you respond? How did you wish you responded? How was Jesus also the victim of friendly fire?

5. Has God ever vindicated you in some way? When that happened, did you thank Him and praise Him? If so, how did it affect your relationship with Him? If not, why not do so now?

For Further Study

Where do *you* see Jesus in Psalm 35? How did Jesus fight the battles we couldn't fight, live the life we couldn't live, and obey the Father in ways we couldn't? Can you give examples from Scripture?

Action Item

Take some time to think about some unfairness you sense in your life right now, or even past unfairness that was never dealt with. Ask God to help you to give these to Him to handle, and let go of them. Ask Him to give you the power you don't have to forgive and let go of bitterness.

If you do not yet know Christ as your Savior, ask Him to come and help you to forgive others as He has forgiven you. Think about what Jesus did for you on the cross and how He forgave and loved you even when you didn't love Him.

Chapter Seven

Gasping in Prayer . . . When You're Drowing in Guilt
(Psalm 38)

1. David acknowledges that God Himself has pierced his heart over his sin. Can you think of a time when God pierced your heart over a sin you had committed or an attitude or behavior you were involved in? Were you surprised by that experience? What did you learn about yourself and about God?

2. Read 1 John 1:9. What does the Bible tell us to do with our guilt over sin? What do you think real confession of sin involves? Is it enough to just tell God that what we have done (or are doing) is wrong, even if we have no intention of abandoning it? What more does God require?

3. Remorse is feeling sorry about the consequences of the sin we are experiencing as a result of our bad behavior. Repentance is feeling sorry that we are the kind of person who would do such a thing. How hard is it to move from remorse to repentance?

4. Is it sometimes hard for you to be brutally honest with God about your sin? What are your fears or apprehensions about admitting to God that you have sinned?

5. How has repentance in your life moved you closer to God? How did it affect the way you felt about God and His concern for you?

For Further Study

Read Hebrews 12:1–11. What can you learn about what God is doing when He brings discipline into our lives? Where else can *you* see Jesus in Psalm 38?

Action Item

There may be an area of sin in your life known only to you and God. It is eating away at you and diminishing your joy. You may have tried to abandon that sin in your own power and failed. Read 2 Corinthians 12:9–10. Ask God to do for you what He did for Paul, to give you the grace and power you lack to overcome this sin. We cannot overcome sin in our own power. Be honest with God and see what He will do. Remember, there are no right words to pray, only honest ones.

Chapter Eight

Gaining Traction When Life Goes off the Rails
(Psalm 40)

1. Has there ever been a time when your life entered a depression, when none of the ways you were formerly able to control were available to you and you couldn't gain any traction? What was that issue, and how did it affect you?

2. In this psalm we see that David really thought about God. He was attentive to what God was doing in his life. How attentive do you think you are to God's activity in your life? How can you recognize His activity in your life?

3. Can you think of something that shows the complex choreography that God orchestrated in your life to accomplish something amazing? What did He have to do? How can you see His hand in it?

4. God often appoints things for us to go through that are difficult but life transforming. They challenge our obedience and faithfulness because they are unpleasant, and we are tempted to complain. What is one time when God used an unpleasant experience to transform you more into the image of Christ? How were you transformed?

5. We all get tired and discouraged at times. Honestly, where do you go first when you are discouraged? Who is your go-to person or guide to help you? In other words, where do you get most of your wisdom for living?

6. Is there something going on in your life right now where you are waiting for God to put your feet on solid ground? How have you approached Him about it? What have you asked for?

For Further Study

Reread Hebrews 10:5–10. How do you see Jesus in the Psalms more clearly through this passage? How do you see the greater David, a greater King, foreshadowed in Psalm 40 as a result of this?

Action Item

Make a concerted effort to share with others the wonderful ways God has met your needs in the past (or even in the present). Publicly proclaim His goodness. In your present difficulty, let Him know what you are struggling with. Pray something like this: "Lord, You delivered me marvelously once, and I praised You then. It's harder to praise You now because my fears would muzzle my praise. But I am going to trust You and ask You to marvelously deliver me once again. And when You do, I promise to praise You again!"

Chapter Nine
The Anatomy of Despair (Psalm 42)

1. During the COVID-19 pandemic, many who used to go to church and be ministered to by the fellowship of the people there found themselves isolated and lonely. Our relationship with God is strengthened by others. Have you ever experienced that loneliness for God, that desiring for God emotionally? What steps have you taken to try to fill that void?

2. Have you ever had someone mock or criticize your faith when you ran into a big obstacle or problem that you couldn't solve? What did they say? How did you respond? How did it make you feel about your relationship with God?

3. Has there ever been a time when you were so low that you considered no longer believing in God? What was that experience, and what happened that made you question God's existence?

4. Have you ever felt free to confess to God the way you feel, even if it's not what you believe? Can you tell God it feels as if He's forgotten you, even if you know He hasn't really? Why or why not?

For Further Study

Where do *you* see Jesus in Psalm 42? How was He overwhelmed emotionally and spiritually—and how did He respond to His heavenly Father?

Action Item

If you are in despair or discouraged, take some time and simply share your honest feelings with God. Don't worry that you might say the wrong thing. Let Him know what you are feeling. He already knows, so you won't be sharing anything with Him that He isn't already aware of. Pray something like, "You know what I am facing, Lord, and I can't fix it. It is tearing me apart, and I am scared to death. Sometimes it feels as if You have forgotten me. Yet I still hope in You and know that I will still praise You. I believe in You still, even though it's hard right now. Meet me here, Lord. Let me sense Your presence."

Chapter Ten

Returning to God . . . from a Long Way Off (Psalm 51)

1. When God reveals sin in our lives to us, it is hard to accept. We want to deny it or keep it hidden, but He insists on exposing it. How can we see God's grace in even this?

2. We all have sins that we regret, of course, but there are certain sins that leave guilt and regret that seem to never quite leave us. We can't believe God could really forgive us of *this*. Is there such a sin in your life right now? What makes it so hard to believe God could really wash you clean of that?

3. We all have sin in our lives. In fact, in your life right now you are struggling with some sin. Take some time and share your sin(s) with God, and be very specific and honest about it. Call it what it is. Don't sugarcoat it.

4. How is every sin cosmic treason? Why is every sin a sin against God first and foremost?

5. Doing good deeds doesn't cancel out any bad ones. We can't work our way out of our sin. How does this show the wisdom of God in having Jesus be the One who cancels out our sins for us?

6. Read 2 Corinthians 5:21 and Colossians 2:14 again. What do these verses tell us that Jesus did to our sins—*all* of them?

For Further Study

Where else do we learn in the Scriptures that Jesus was the final and eternal sacrifice who takes away our sin? How can we see in this psalm a picture of Jesus, who rescues us from a long way off?

Action Item

Each of us has a sin, either minor (in our eyes) or major, at this moment. All sin affects our fellowship with God (but not our *relationship* with God if we are Christians). God wants to draw you nearer to Him, but this sin is causing spiritual and emotional distance. Using your own words, and even some of David's, ask God to draw you nearer to Him and to help you jettison the sinful attitudes and behaviors that are hurting your fellowship. Be painfully honest. Remember, Jesus is your advocate with the Father on your behalf. He is helping you in ways you can't even understand as you come to the Father in repentance.

Chapter Eleven

Bridging Our Distance from God (Psalm 53)

1. Read Psalm 14 and compare it with Psalm 53. What are the similarities you see, and what are the differences? Why do you think God put both these psalms, which are so similar, in the Psalter?

2. If you did not believe in God, were you arrogant about it or just quietly accepting of the fact, with no animosity to others who disagreed? What do you think prompted either response in you?

3. Did you ever have a designer god in your life? If so, what was this god like, and how did this god reflect your own desires and expectations of deity?

4. The Bible makes it very clear that (1) there are many who are lost and rebelling against God, and (2) that fact breaks His heart. Have you ever reflected that heart of God in your prayers for others, especially those who are hostile to Him? Take some time now and create a list of two or three people you can lift to God in prayer, and ask Him to bring them home to Him. God loves it when we begin to echo His own heart back to Him.

For Further Study

David longs for salvation to come out of Zion. Explain from the Scriptures how God actually did create a Bridge for us to cross over from death to life. In what way was Jesus that Bridge between God and man? What other ways do you see Jesus in this psalm?

Action Item

Our salvation is indeed the result of a prisoner exchange. Jesus's life was exchanged for our own on the cross. He took the punishment while we gained the freedom. There will never be enough words to thank Him for this, but God never tires of hearing our thanks. Take time now and thank God that you have been forgiven, accepted, adopted, and born again into newness of life. Confess your deepest thanks and praise.

If you have not yet received Christ as your Savior, you now see that Jesus is the Bridge. You need to cross over to the Father through Him, and He works on your behalf. He has made it possible for you to have peace with the Father through canceling out all your sins. He is waiting with open arms. Will you ask Him to enter your life and receive Him as your Lord and Savior today?

Chapter Twelve

Accessing God's Protection under Intense Fire (Psalm 56)

1. Are you in some kind of danger? Do you worry about how you are going to get out of a particular situation or how it might end? Have you actually shared that fear with God? Do that now. Maybe write it out to help you better organize your thoughts.

2. Some of the most painful experiences we have are conflicts with people. They hurt more and go deeper. Think about some ways in which people have trampled on you in your past or even in your present. Who did you typically turn to in such times for help?

3. Have you ever put your trust in God to help you and felt peace, then later experienced that same fear pop back up? Did it make you question your faith—or God?

4. David laments how people "distort my words." How does that happen today in our culture? Have you ever had your ideas or thoughts misrepresented by others? How did it make you feel?

5. David says that God has "put my tears in Your bottle." Explain how that idea affects you as you think about it. What does it tell you about God and what He feels toward us?

6. Our government, companies, and even friends promise us various things, and when we don't feel they are delivering, we feel free to remind them. Are you reminding God of His promise to protect and deliver you in the midst of your current stress? What promises of God can you think of that you can quote back to God in prayer?

For Further Study

Where do *you* see Jesus in Psalm 56? What other Scriptures can you think of that talk about the inevitability of trials and testings in your life? What do those Scriptures tell us the purpose of trials and testings is?

Action Item

Spend time with God in prayer, asking Him to protect you in the danger you are facing. Ask Him to help you remember how He has delivered you in the past. Be honest about how you are feeling but also how you want to trust Him. Confess that your faith is weak and fragile, and ask Him to strengthen it through His Holy Spirit and His Word. Use some of David's words if it helps, but also use your own. Then consciously decide to listen to God and His Word, and allow that to lessen the other voices of fear you hear.

Chapter Thirteen
You Are the Object of His Attention (Psalm 139)

1. We have a fear of letting people get too close to us or knowing too much about us. Why do you think that is true? What are we worried about?

2. How does the idea that you have God's perpetually undivided attention affect you? Why is it hard to believe, and how does it bring comfort and encouragement?

3. Hebrews 4:13 tells us that "there is no creature hidden from His sight, but all things are open and laid bare to the eyes of Him with whom we have to do." When it comes to your relationship with God, what are some of the "all things" that are open and laid bare before Him?

4. There are times when things God does cause awe in us and prompt worship and thanks. Take some time and think of ways in which you are in awe of God and what He has done or who He is in some way. Then share that awe in confession and prayer to God. Use some of David's words if they are helpful, but also use your own.

5. David wasn't just thankful that there was a great God but that God allowed David to experience His greatness by the way he had been created. What are some of the senses God has given us which enable us to be aware of His greatness?

6. David writes, "How precious also are Your thoughts to me, O God! How vast is the sum of them! If I should count them, they would outnumber the sand." From what this psalm, and the rest of the Bible, tells us, what are the thoughts that you know God has toward you constantly? List as many as you can. How does that knowledge encourage you?

For Further Study

Where else do you see Jesus in Psalm 139? Reread Psalm 139. What are additional insights you have gained about how deeply and intimately God is acquainted with you? What stands out as most powerful and encouraging to you?

Action Item

Ask God to search your heart, and give Him permission to highlight and purge from your life and heart all the things that will inevitably hurt you and your relationship with Him. Ask God to show you even more ways that He is intimately involved with your life, that your trust in Him would grow. Ask Him to reveal His works in your life to you.

What David ultimately wanted was for God to "lead me in the everlasting way." If you have never given your life to Christ, that is what God wants to do for you, to lead you in the everlasting way, the way that leads to eternal life. That's why Jesus came. Just honestly ask God to lead you in the everlasting way, and He will!

Bibliography and Special Thanks

Whenever one endeavors to write a book on any part of the Bible, one inevitably owes a deep debt to those who have gone before and studied the book. We all stand on the shoulders of those who have been led by the Holy Spirit and done the arduous work of exegeting the text. Within each commentary are also the insights of so many others the authors quoted, enriching the book even more.

Their insights have helped to form mine. While I have been careful to cite works when I quote them directly, every book added to my understanding. With that in mind, the following books were indispensable to my study:

The Bible. It all starts here.

John Calvin, *Commentary on the Psalms*, ed. David C. Searle (East Peoria, IL: Versa Press, 2009).

John Goldingay, *Psalms, Volume 1: Psalms 1–41* (Grand Rapids, MI: Baker Academic, 2006).

Henry Ironside, *Studies on Book One of the Psalms* (Neptune, NJ: Loizeaux Brothers, 1976).

Timothy and Kathy Keller, *The Songs of Jesus: A Year of Daily Devotions in the Psalms* (New York, NY: Viking, 2015).

Derek Kidner, *Psalms 1–72* (Downers Grove, IL: IVP Academic, 1973).

———, *Psalms 73–150* (Downers Grove, IL: IVP Academic, 2008).

Tremper Longman III, *Psalms*, Tyndale Old Testament Commentaries (Downers Grove, IL: IVP Academic, 2014).

Allen P. Ross, *A Commentary on the Psalms: 1–41* (Grand Rapids, MI: Kregel Academic, 2011).

Charles Spurgeon, John Calvin, and Matthew Henry, *The Parallel Classic Commentary on the Psalms* (Chattanooga, TN: AMG Publishers, 2005).

Charles R. Swindoll, *Living the Psalms: Living the Psalms: Encouragement for the Daily Grind* (Franklin, TN: Worthy Publishing, 2012).

Notes

CHAPTER 1: Honest to God

1. Timothy and Kathy Keller, *The Songs of Jesus: A Year of Daily Devotions in the Psalms* (New York: Viking, 2015), vii.

2. Albert Barnes, *Barnes' Notes on the Old Testament: Psalms* (Grand Rapids, MI: Baker Books, 1996), xiii.

3. Athanasius, as quoted in John Goldingay, *Psalms, Volume 1: Psalms 1–41* (Grand Rapids, MI: Baker Academic, 2006), 9.

4. Martin Luther, as quoted in Tremper Longman III, *Psalms*, Tyndale Old Testament Commentaries (Downers Grove, IL: InterVarsity Press, 2014), 9.

5. Allen P. Ross, *A Commentary on the Psalms: 1–41* (Grand Rapids, MI: Kregel Academic, 2011), 27.

6. Henry A. Ironside, *Studies on Book One of the Psalms* (Neptune, NJ: Loizeaux Brothers Inc., 1952), 4–5.

7. Goldingay, *Psalms*, 22.

8. Keller, *Songs of Jesus*, viii.

9. Walter Brueggemann, *The Message of the Psalms: A Theological Commentary* (Minneapolis, MN: Augsburg Publishing House, 1984), 15.

10. J. Sidlow Baxter, "The Book of Psalms," in *Explore the Book* (Grand Rapids, MI: Zondervan, 2010), 83.

11. Baxter, "The Book of Psalms," 83.

12. Bruce Waltke, as quoted in Longman, *Psalms*, xx.

13. N. T. Wright, *The Case for the Psalms: Why They Are Essential* (San Francisco: HarperOne, 2016), 110.

14. Baxter, "The Book of Psalms," 86.

15. Athanasius, as quoted in Goldingay, 22–23.

CHAPTER 2: Setting Up a Living Trust

1. Franklin Delano Roosevelt, "FDR Nothing to Fear but Fear Itself 1933 Inaugural Address," Donald Pohlmeyer, September 23, 2013, video, 1:47, YouTube, https://www.youtube.com/watch?v=nHFTtz3uucY.

CHAPTER 3: Sin and Its Discontents

1. *Merriam-Webster*, s.v. "pine (*v.*)," accessed October 13, 2022, https://www.merriam-webster.com/dictionary/pine.

2. C. S. Lewis, *The Problem of Pain* (New York: MacMillan Publishing Company, 1962), 156.

3. Timothy Keller, *Counterfeit Gods: The Empty Promises of Love, Money, Sex, and Power, and the Only Hope That Matters* (New York: Penguin Books, 2009), 164.

4. Charles Spurgeon, John Calvin, and Matthew Henry, *Parallel Classic Commentary on the Psalms* (Chattanooga, TN: AMG Publishers, 2005), 18.

CHAPTER 4: The Question Everyone Wants to Ask God

1. Margaret Manning Shull, "Deus Absconditus," iDisciple, accessed October 8, 2022, https://www.idisciple.org/post/deus-absconditus.

2. Philip Yancey, "National Tragedy and the Empty Tomb," *Christianity Today*, March 28, 2013, https://www.christianitytoday.com/ct/2013/april/national-tragedy-and-empty-tomb.html.

3. C. S. Lewis, as quoted in William Griffin, *Clive Staples Lewis: A Dramatic Life* (San Francisco: Harper & Row, 1986), 76.

4. C. S. Lewis, *Christian Reflections* (Grand Rapids, MI: Eerdmans Publishing, 1995), 41–43.

CHAPTER 5: Joy Comes in the Morning

1. Joni Eareckson Tada, "Reflections on the 50th Anniversary of My Diving Accident," The Gospel Coalition, July 30, 2017, https://www.thegospelcoalition.org/article/reflections-on-50th-anniversary-of-my-diving-accident/.

2. Timothy and Kathy Keller, *The Songs of Jesus: A Year of Daily Devotions in the Psalms* (New York: Viking, 2015), 54.

3. Sara Bibel, "5 Little-Known Facts about How J. K. Rowling Brought Harry Potter to Life," Biography, updated May 13, 2020, https://www.biography.com/news/jk-rowling-harry-potter-facts.

4. "How Dr. Seuss Got His Start 'on Mulberry Street,'" NPR, January 24, 2012, https://www.npr.org/2012/01/24/145471724/how-dr-seuss-got-his-start-on-mulberry-street.

CHAPTER 6: Seeking Vindication

1. Rachael Denhollander, "Rachael Denhollander Gives Powerful, Final Victim Statement in Nassar Sentencing," WXYZ-TV Detroit Channel 7, January 24, 2018, video, 36:04, https://www.youtube.com/watch?v=2nEvHeEUnVE.

2. Timothy and Kathy Keller, *The Songs of Jesus: A Year of Daily Devotions in the Psalms* (New York: Viking, 2015), 67.

3. Dante Hosseini, "The Cathedral That Defeated Stalin," *The Stream*, December 4, 2015, https://stream.org/cathedral-defeated-stalin/.

4. Henry Ironside, *Studies on Book One of the Psalms* (Neptune, NJ: Loizeaux Brothers Inc., 1952), 210.

CHAPTER 7: Gasping in Prayer . . . When You're Drowning in Guilt

1. Tremper Longman III, *Psalms*, Tyndale Old Testament Commentaries (Downers Grove, IL: InterVarsity Press, 2014), 183.

CHAPTER 8: Gaining Traction When Life Goes off the Rails

1. Henry Ironside, *Studies on Book One of the Psalms* (Neptune, NJ: Loizeaux Brothers Inc., 1952), 232.

2. John Piper, "A Call to Love—and to Death," Desiring God, June 25, 1995, https://www.desiringgod.org/messages/a-call-to-love-and-to-death.

CHAPTER 9: The Anatomy of Despair

1. Kimberli Lira, "Why the Church Doesn't Need Any More Coffee Bars," For Every Mom, March 13, 2017, https://foreverymom.com/faith/why-the-church -doesnt-need-any-more-coffee-bars-kimberli-lira/.

2. Charles R. Swindoll, *Living the Psalms: Encouragement for the Daily Grind* (Franklin, TN: Worthy Publishing, 2012), 119–20.

3. Charles H. Spurgeon, "Intercessory Prayer," in *The Metropolitan Tabernacle Pulpit Sermons*, vol. 7 (London: Passmore & Alabaster, 1861), 449.

4. Sheldon Vanauken, *A Severe Mercy* (San Francisco: HarperSanFrancisco, 2009).

5. Richard Wurmbrand, as quoted in Drew Dyck, *Yawning at Tigers: You Can't Tame God, So Stop Trying* (Nashville: Thomas Nelson Publishing 2014), 153.

CHAPTER 10: Returning to God . . . from a Long Way Off

1. Thomas Tarrants, "I Was a Violent Klansman Who Deserved to Die," *Christianity Today*, August 19, 2019, https://www.christianitytoday.com/ct/2019/september/thomas-tarrants-consumed-hate-redeemed-love-klansman.html.

2. *The Collected Letters of C. S. Lewis*, ed. Walter Hooper, vol. 2, *Books, Broadcasts, and the War, 1931–1949* (Cambridge, England: Cambridge University Press, 2004), 122.

3. Tim Keller, *The Prodigal Prophet: Jonah and the Mystery of God's Mercy* (New York: Viking, 2018), 138–39.

4. Derek Kidner, *Psalms 1–72*, Tyndale Old Testament Commentaries (Downers Grove, IL: InterVarsity Press, 1973), 194.

CHAPTER 11: Bridging Our Distance from God

1. Derek Kidner, *Psalms 1–72*, Tyndale Old Testament Commentaries (Downers Grove, IL: InterVarsity Press, 1973), 95.

2. Tremper Longman III, *Psalms*, Tyndale Old Testament Commentaries (Downers Grove, IL: InterVarsity Press, 2014), 99.

3. Michele Crowe and Gabriele Moss, "6 Women Reveal Why They Became Satanists," Bustle, October 25, 2017, https://www.bustle.com/p/6-women-reveal-why-they-became-satanists-2984953.

4. Aleksandr Solzhenitsyn, "Notable Quotations," The Aleksandr Solzhenitsyn Center, accessed February 21, 2023, https://www.solzhenitsyncenter.org/notable-quotations.

5. The location has been omitted and names have been changed to protect this family.

6. Tim Keller, *The Prodigal Prophet: Jonah and the Mystery of God's Mercy* (New York: Viking, 2018), *Prodigal Prophet*, 143–45.

7. John Stott, *The Cross of Christ* (Downers Grove, IL: InterVarsity Press, 1986), 159–60.

CHAPTER 12: Accessing God's Protection under Intense Fire

1. Desmond Doss, as quoted in Elizabeth Blair, "The Real 'Hacksaw Ridge' Soldier Saved 75 Souls without Ever Carrying a Gun," NPR, November 4, 2016, https://www.npr.org/2016/11/04/500548745/the-real-hacksaw-ridge-soldier -saved-75-souls-without-ever-carrying-a-gun; and Eliza Berman, "The True Story behind *Hacksaw Ridge*," *Time*, November 3, 2016, https://time.com/4539373 /hacksaw-ridge-movie-true-story/.

2. Blair, "The Real 'Hacksaw Ridge' Soldier."

3. Derek Kidner, *Psalms 1–72*, Tyndale Old Testament Commentaries (Downers Grove, IL: InterVarsity Press, 1973), 42.

4. John MacArthur, *The MacArthur Bible Commentary* (Nashville: Thomas Nelson Publishers, 2005), 636.

5. Allen P. Ross, "Psalms," in *The Bible Knowledge Commentary*, ed. John F. Walvoord and Roy B. Zuck (Wheaton, IL: Victor Books, 1986), 835.

6. Kidner, *Psalms 1–72*, 38.

7. Eugene Merrill, "1 Samuel," in *The Bible Knowledge Commentary*, 451.

8. George MacDonald, *The Princess and the Goblin* (London: Puffin Classics, 2010), 103–4. First published 1872.

9. Betsy Childs Howard, "Ghost Army," The Gospel Coalition, June 11, 2014, https://www.thegospelcoalition.org/article/ghost-army/.

10. Abraham Lincoln, as quoted in Michael Medved, *The American Miracle: Divine Providence in the Rise of the Republic* (New York: Crown Forum, 2016), 319.

CHAPTER 13: You Are the Object of His Attention

1. Annie Johnson Flint, "Pressed," in *He Giveth More Grace: One Hundred Poems by Annie Johnson Flint* (self-pub., Hayden Press, 2020), 12.

2. Charles R. Swindoll, *Living the Psalms: Encouragement for the Daily Grind* (Franklin, TN: Worthy Publishing, 2012), 276.

3. Jon Hamilton, "Think You're Multitasking? Think Again," NPR, October 2, 2008, https://www.npr.org/2008/10/02/95256794/think-youre-multitasking-think -again.

4. Derek Kidner, *Psalms 73–150* (Downers Grove, IL: IVP Academic, 2008), 504.

Help us get the word out!

Our Daily Bread Publishing exists to feed the soul with the Word of God.

If you appreciated this book, please let others know.

- Pick up another copy to give as a gift.
- Share a link to the book or mention it on social media.
- Write a review on your blog, on a book-seller's website, or at our own site (odb.org/store).
- Recommend this book for your church, book club, or small group.

Connect with us:

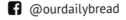 @ourdailybread

 @ourdailybread

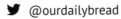 @ourdailybread

Our Daily Bread Publishing
PO Box 3566
Grand Rapids, Michigan 49501 USA

✉ books@odb.org